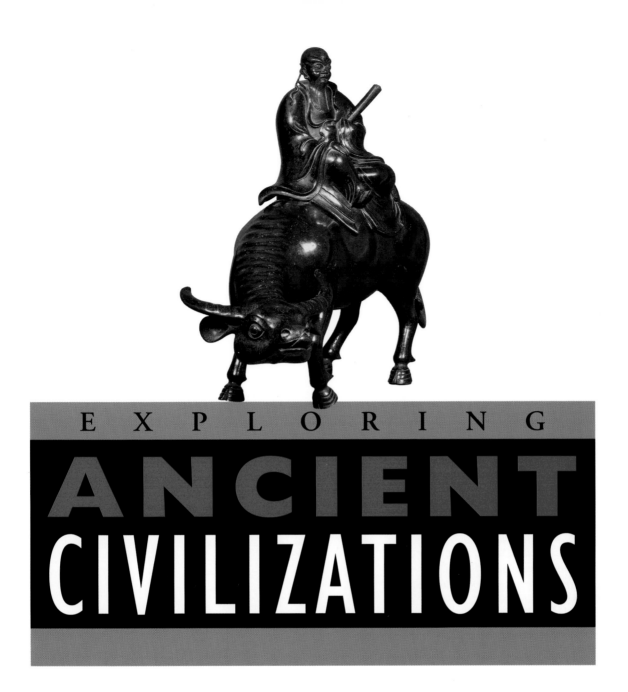

EXPLORING ANCIENT CIVILIZATIONS

3

Chavín – Dong Son Culture

Marshall Cavendish

Marshall Cavendish
99 White Plains Road
Tarrytown, New York 10591-9001

www.marshallcavendish.com

© 2004 Marshall Cavendish Corporation

Consultants: Daud Ali, School of Oriental and African
Studies, University of London; Michael Brett, School
of Oriental and African Studies, London; John
Chinnery, School of Oriental and African Studies,
London; Philip de Souza; Joann Fletcher; Anthony
Green; Peter Groff, Department of Philosophy,
Bucknell University; Mark Handley, History
Department, University College London; Anders
Karlsson, School of Oriental and African Studies,
London; Alan Leslie, Glasgow University Archaeology
Research Department; Michael E. Smith, Department
of Anthropology, University at Albany; Matthew
Spriggs, Head of School of Archaeology and
Anthropology, Australian National University

Contributing authors: Richard Balkwill, Richard
Burrows, Peter Chrisp, Richard Dargie, Steve Eddy,
Clive Gifford, Jen Green, Peter Hicks, Robert Hull,
Jonathan Ingoldby, Pat Levy, Steven Maddocks, John
Malam, Saviour Pirotta, Stewart Ross, Sean Sheehan,
Jane Shuter

Library of Congress Cataloging-in-Publication Data
Exploring ancient civilizations.
    p. cm.
Includes bibliographical references and indexes.
  ISBN 0-7614-7456-0 (set : alk. paper) -- ISBN 0-7614-7457-9 (v. 1 :
alk. paper) -- ISBN 0-7614-7458-7 (v. 2 : alk. paper) -- ISBN
0-7614-7459-5 (v. 3 : alk. paper) -- ISBN 0-7614-7460-9 (v. 4 : alk.
paper) -- ISBN 0-7614-7461-7 (v. 5 : alk. paper) -- ISBN 0-7614-7462-5
(v. 6 : alk. paper) -- ISBN 0-7614-7463-3 (v. 7 : alk. paper) -- ISBN
0-7614-7464-1 (v. 8 : alk. paper) -- ISBN 0-7614-7465-X (v. 9 : alk.
paper) -- ISBN 0-7614-7466-8 (v. 10 : alk. paper) -- ISBN 0-7614-7467-6
(v. 11 : alk. paper)
  1. Civilization, Ancient--Encyclopedias.
CB311.E97 2004
930'.03--dc21
                                         2003041224

ISBN 0-7614-7456-0 (set)
ISBN 0-7614-7459-5 (vol. 3)

Printed and bound in China

07 06 05 04 03 5 4 3 2 1

WHITE-THOMSON PUBLISHING
Editor: Alex Woolf
Design: Derek Lee
Picture Research: Glass Onion Pictures
Cartographer: Peter Bull Design
Indexer: Fiona Barr

MARSHALL CAVENDISH
Editor: Thomas McCarthy
Editorial Director: Paul Bernabeo
Production Manager: Michael Esposito

Contents

Chavín

The Chavín lived 2,500 years ago in Peru. Experts do not know exactly when this culture started, but they do know that Chavín settlements near Peru's coast existed before 900 BCE and that its main religious center, at Chavín de Huantár, flourished between the ninth and third centuries BCE. The Chavín have left behind many impressive artifacts and are considered the first highly developed culture to be found in Peru.

The Early Horizon

Northern Peru is divided into three quite different stretches of land, each running north to south and each with its own climate. The coastal area, which is desert-like, is bordered by the cooler northern highlands made up of the towering peaks of the Andes. Farther inland the land slopes down into tropical rain forest. Before the Chavín the geography of Peru appeared to keep peoples isolated from one another in one of these strips of land. The Chavín period is called the Early Horizon, because its influence was felt by peoples in all three geographic areas of northern Peru.

Chavín de Huantár

Deep in Peru's northern highlands lie the ruins of Chavín de Huantár, the biggest ceremonial and religious center of its time in Peru. This place has given its name to the Chavín culture and features many of its most impressive artifacts. Chavín de Huantár is divided into two areas – a central area holding temple buildings and a residential area where people lived. Despite being over two thousand years old, the buildings in the 1,500-foot (457 m) square central area are relatively well preserved. Many of its impressive stone carvings can still be seen.

Metalworking

The Chavín's metalworking tools – stone hammers, stones with sharp edges acting as cutters, and bones sharpened to a point to make an awl – were simple but effective. Beautiful gold and silver plaques, drinking vessels, and jewelry were adorned with intricate designs, often of jaguars, crocodiles, and other creatures. The Chavín started to work with gold just after 600 BCE. They proved to be gifted goldsmiths, learning not only how to hammer

▼ *A map of the ceremonial and religious site of Chavín de Huantár.*

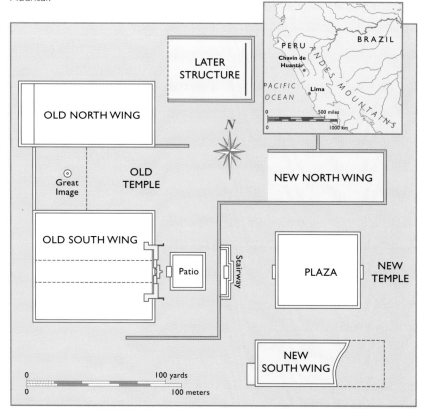

CHAVÍN ART

The Chavín were impressive artists, carving stone, producing and decorating pottery, and weaving and painting cloth. They produced textiles and clothing patterned with what is called the resist style of painting, similar to modern-day tie-dyeing. Their pottery was often decorated with figures of warriors and animals such as birds, monkeys, alligators, and snakes. The most common subject of all was the head of a big cat with fangs, which archaeologists believe was modeled on the jaguar. These decorations were all religious; the animal pictures were actually paintings of their gods.

CHAVIN	
1800–900 BCE Initial period.	**400 BCE** Roads and trading routes developed.
900–200 BCE Early Horizon period.	**400–250 BCE** Height of Chavín culture.
850 BCE Earliest settlement at Chavín de Huantár.	**300–200 BCE** Decline of Chavín culture.

◄ This Chavín ceramic vessel has two tubes joining the main part of the container to its opening at the top. Called a stirrup spout vessel and decorated with a head, it dates from between 1000 and 600 BCE. Other stirrup spout vessels feature carvings of serpents and jaguars.

out thin sheets of metal but also how to use heat to solder these sheets together to form three-dimensional objects.

Rise and Fall

The height of Chavín influence started around 400 BCE, when there was a great expansion in building at Chavín de Huantár. Less than two hundred years later new building work halted. The Chavín styles of metalwork and pottery disapeared as well. No one knows why the Chavín declined, but many centuries passed before another culture dominated the region.

THE OLD TEMPLE

▼ This example of stonework from inside the temple at Chavín de Huantár has a regular pattern of snake fangs running through its middle and below it a carved pattern of animal claws.

In the center of Chavín de Huantár lies an impressive building that was first known as the Castillo, meaning "castle," but is now called the Old Temple. It is believed to have been the most important ceremonial site in Peru during the time of the Chavín. The Old Temple is over thirty feet high and built of heavy, rectangular stone blocks. It contains a number of rooms and galleries linked by a maze of dim, narrow passageways. Throughout the interior beautiful as well as frightening stone carvings of mythical creatures, big cats, and humans can be found on walls and on pillars.

In the oldest part of the temple stands the most remarkable statue. It is a single shaft of granite standing almost fifteen feet high and weighing approximately two tons. It appears to be part human, part jaguar, and part serpent or snake. It has clawed feet, humanlike hands, snakes or serpents for hair, and two giant fangs. Originally known as El Lanzón, or the Smiling God, it is now called the Great Image because it is believed to have been the main object that the Chavín people worshiped.

One room in the Old Temple that has been excavated by archaeologists is called the Gallery of the Offerings. Among the remains found there were almost eight hundred pots. Some of this pottery appears to come from peoples who lived between 150 and 250 miles (240–400 km) away. This discovery suggests that long-distance pilgrimages were made to Chavín de Huantár to leave offerings of food and drink, carried in these pots, for the gods.

SEE ALSO
- Moche Culture
- Olmec

Cheng

Cheng (also known as Zheng or Qin Shi Huangdi) was a Chinese prince who was born around 259 BCE and ruled as emperor of China from 221 to 210 BCE. During his brief reign he unified China under a strong system of government that was to last for two thousand years.

War and Conquest

Cheng was prince of the Chinese state of Qin, which lay in present-day northwest China. In 247 BCE he became ruler of Qin at the young age of nine. At this time Qin was one of a patchwork of states in China, each ruled by its own lord and constantly at war with one another.

Around 234 BCE Cheng began a campaign to conquer the rest of China. He became known as the "tiger of Qin" because of his ruthless campaigns. By 221 his triumph was complete, and Cheng declared himself Qin Shi Huangdi, the first Qin emperor. Qin, pronounced "chin," became China, the name of his new empire.

A Harsh Ruler

Cheng established his capital at Xianyang in northern China. He forced his defeated rivals to attend the imperial court so that he could keep watch on them and make sure they did not cause trouble. Cheng was a harsh ruler who did not take kindly to criticism. When scholars criticized his rule and used history books and literature to support their arguments, Cheng ordered all such books to be burned.

Cheng ruled his vast new empire by setting up an efficient system of administration. He divided the country into provinces, each governed by an important civil servant and a military commander. He ordered a standard system of weights and measures and the same coinage to be used everywhere. Everyone had to speak the same language and use one script for writing. All these measures remained in place long after his death.

▼ The emperor Cheng ruled with an iron hand, executing all scholars who did not agree with him and burning their books.

Cheng also improved communications throughout his empire by building roads and canals. He ordered the building of the Great Wall of China to defend his empire from the nomadic tribes to the north. Tens of thousands of peasants were ordered from their fields to help with its construction. Heavy taxes were imposed on everyone to help pay for this project.

Cheng's Legacy

Cheng died in 209 BCE at the age of fifty. He was succeeded by his son, who proved to be a weak ruler. Just one year after Cheng's death, civil war broke out. Peasants rose up against the harsh rule of the Qin and united under a minor official named Liu Bang. By 202 the Qin dynasty was overthrown and Liu Bang became Emperor Gaozu. Gaozu took over Cheng's efficient administration. The idea of a unified Chinese empire, which Cheng had created, lasted for over two thousand years.

SEE ALSO
- China
- Great Wall of China

▼ *Part of the army of terra-cotta soldiers that guarded Cheng's tomb.*

CHENG'S TOMB AND THE "TERRA-COTTA ARMY"

Cheng is probably most famous for the lavish tomb he had built as his memorial. This vast underground palace was constructed on Mount Li, which lies about twenty-five miles (40 km) east of the present-day city of Xi'an. Nearby are vast underground chambers containing seven thousand life-size terra-cotta (pottery) statues of warriors, who were intended to guard the emperor in the afterlife. Each statue has a different face, perhaps the likeness of a real soldier. This amazing tomb was discovered by accident in 1974 by farmers digging a well.

Children

Life in many ancient civilizations centered around the family. Parents looked forward to having children. The poor prayed they would have boys who could help their father in his work and continue the family trade when he became ill. In many cultures girls, who would need a dowry when they got married, were often abandoned outdoors and left to die in the cold.

Birth

The mortality rate in the ancient world was very high. Mothers as well as children frequently died during childbirth, and infants that survived childbirth often succumbed to deadly diseases. The birth of a healthy child was therefore celebrated with joy and feasting. In Pompei the family would paint a sign on the front of their house telling everyone that a new child had arrived. Greek families pinned an olive branch to the front door if they had a boy, a tuft of wool if they had a girl. The proud father would dance around the hearth with the baby in his arms. He would thank Hestia, the goddess of the hearth, for sending him a healthy child.

Schooling

In ancient times only the children of the rich and privileged went to school. In Mesopotamia priests ran the schools. Rich boys who wanted to become priests or scribes attended formal schools. They learned reading, writing, medicine, astrology, religion, and law. Students had access to libraries, which were usually part of a temple.

Ancient Egyptian schools were generally run by priests. Future scribes and priests started their education between the ages of five and ten. Their studies included reading, writing, mathematics, literature, and music, as well as sports. When they were considered ready, Egyptian students also began practical training in the temples or the offices where they would work as adults.

▼ *This fifth-century-BCE red-figure cup shows scenes of Greek children at school. Some pupils are learning to play the flute and the harp. A teacher is showing a student how to write on a clay tablet with a stylus. The child in the lower picture is reading from a scroll.*

By 500 BCE education in the Greek city-state of Sparta focused on teaching boys how to be soldiers. At the age of seven, boys were required to live in soldiers' barracks, which were also their schools. Teachers encouraged the boys to steal food, but if they were caught, they were beaten in front of their classmates. Children in the city-state of Athens had a different kind of education. The pupils were taught literacy, physical education, and the appreciation of the great poets and historians, especially Homer.

In ancient Rome most children were taught at home. Before the sixth century BCE wealthy parents would teach their offspring the customs of their country. The father would show them how to run the estate and look after the slaves. Later, families hired tutors to look after their children. Most in demand were Greek slaves who could teach the Greek language as well as rhetoric, that is, the art of speaking effectively. From around the third century BCE rich Roman children could also go to school.

Boys, and sometimes girls, would attend classes with a tutor called a *magister ludi*. Pupils read from scrolls and wrote on wax-coated tablets with a stylus. At the age of twelve or thirteen, rich children moved up to another type of school where they had lessons in Latin and Greek literature, astronomy, and geometry.

Toys

By 2000 BCE toddlers in the Indus valley were playing with toy carts pulled by miniature bulls. Children in ancient Egypt had wooden animals that moved on wheels. Wooden animals with movable parts were also popular.

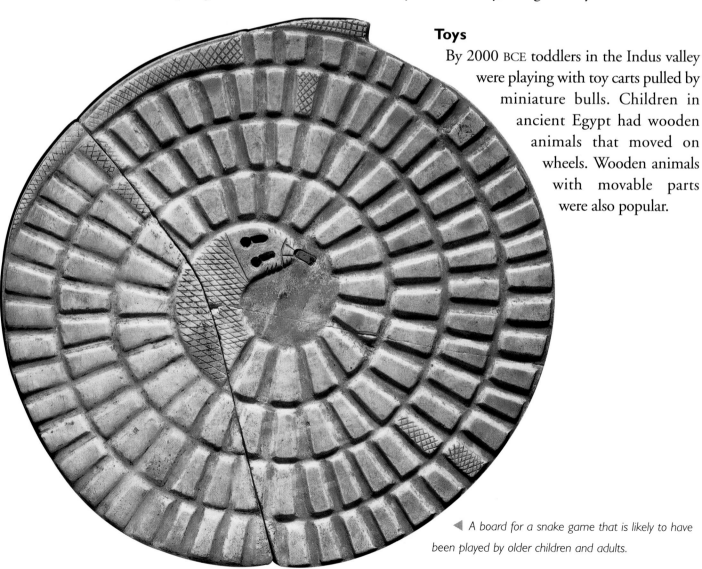

◀ A board for a snake game that is likely to have been played by older children and adults.

Egyptian girls played with wooden dolls as well as stuffed dolls with their own linen dresses. In Greece many dolls were made of clay, while Roman girls had stuffed rag dolls. One found in a grave dates back to the third or fourth century BCE.

Blindman's buff was very popular in ancient Rome. Roman children called it *chalke muia*, which means "the brazen fly." Greek children played hopscotch. The idea of hopping around a pattern of squares was probably inspired by the Greek myths, which featured mazes. Tic-tac-toe was a popular game in ancient Egypt, Greece, China, and Rome.

Growing Up

Childhood did not last very long in the ancient world. By the age of seven, many would be preparing for their lives as adults. Roman boys became fully fledged citizens at the age of sixteen or seventeen, although they could marry at the age of fourteen. Roman girls, like their Egyptian counterparts, could marry when they were twelve.

On the day a boy became a Roman citizen, he put away his bulla – a locket given to him at birth – and put on a white tunic, helped ceremoniously by his father. It was a sign that he was now a man. A girl would give her bulla to her father the day before her wedding. Toys were handed down to the younger children.

▶ *This stone carving from ancient Rome marks a child's grave and shows a boy wearing a bulla around his neck. These charms were given to boys by their fathers.*

SEE ALSO
- Babylonians • Education • Egypt • Greece, Classical • Hebrews • Mesopotamia
- Roman Republic and Empire

THE FOLLOWING IS FROM A LETTER SENT BY DIOGENES, A WOMAN LIVING IN EGYPT IN THE THIRD CENTURY CE, TO HER BROTHER ALEXANDER WHOSE WIFE HAS JUST HAD A BABY:

Many greetings to little Theon. Eight toys have been brought for him, and these I send to you.

China

China is one of the world's earliest civilizations, dating back at least five thousand years. The earliest written records in China were produced around 1500 BCE. Early Chinese kings ruled only a small part of the territory now occupied by China. In 221 BCE, however, China became a unified empire, which gradually became larger.

The Chinese empire two thousand years ago covered an area approximately the size of Europe. It was bounded by deserts and mountains to the north and west and by oceans to the east. The Chinese called it Zhongguo, which means "Middle Kingdom," because they believed it lay at the center of the civilized world.

Prehistoric Times

Archaeologists have found evidence of prehistoric humans in China that are over 500,000 years old. Much later, by around 25,000 years ago, Chinese people were using shell ornaments and stone tools. Around five thousand years ago Chinese civilization began to develop along the banks of the mighty Yellow River (the Huang He) in northeast China. Farmers began to raise crops in the fertile soil of the river valley, and settlements sprang up that later grew into towns and cities. Civilization gradually spread south to the Yangzi, another great river in east-central China.

The First Chinese Kings

Chinese history is usually divided into dynasties, periods during which China was governed by a single ruling family. The first dynasty of which written records survive was the Shang, which ruled northern China from around 1700 to 1122 BCE. The Shang was replaced by the Zhou, a dynasty of warrior kings from the west who ruled China for more than 850 years, until 256 BCE.

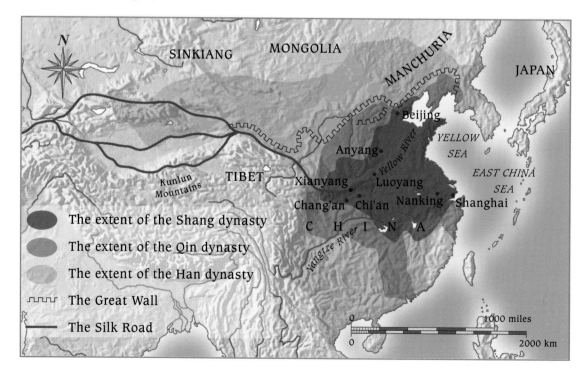

▶ This map shows the boundaries of the territory ruled by the Shang, Qin, and Han dynasties, the Great Wall of China, and the trading route with the West, known as the Silk Road.

The extent of the Shang dynasty
The extent of the Qin dynasty
The extent of the Han dynasty
The Great Wall
The Silk Road

WU DI *141–87 BCE*

The Han emperor Wu Di founded a university for civil servants. The main subject of study was the works of Confucius, a great Chinese philosopher. Students had to pass final examinations in Confucian thought to become government officials. In 138 BCE, Wu Di sent an army west to conquer what is now Afghanistan, and a vast new region became part of China. On the campaign Chinese commanders were surprised to learn that other highly developed civilizations existed beyond China's borders in the far west.

CHINA

1700s–1122 BCE Shang dynasty rules northern China.	**221–207 BCE** Qin dynasty establishes the Chinese empire.
1122–256 BCE Zhou dynasty.	**206 BCE–220 CE** Han dynasty.
500s BCE Confucianism and Taoism founded.	**220–581 CE** Period of disunity.
500s–221 BCE Warring States period.	**518–618 CE** Sui dynasty reunites China.

The last few centuries of Zhou rule were a time of turmoil in China. Royal control weakened as rival princes challenged the authority of the Zhou. This period, known as the Warring States period, was ended by a warrior prince named Cheng.

Sons of Heaven

In 221 BCE Cheng, ruler of the Qin, defeated the other princes and established the first Chinese empire, which covered what is now eastern and central China. Successive emperors built on his achievements, and the empire gradually expanded.

Chinese emperors called themselves the Sons of Heaven. They believed that the gods had appointed them to rule over the vast nation. Cheng established a strong central government and launched several major building projects, including the Great Wall of China. However, his people found him a harsh ruler who would not tolerate any opposition.

▼ *This bronze jug, shaped in the form of an owl and tiger, dates from the Shang dynasty, around 1300 BCE. It was probably used in religious ceremonies.*

In 206 BCE Qin rule was overthrown by a new dynasty, the Han, which governed China for the next four centuries, until 220 CE. The Han took over the civil service that Cheng had set up to run his empire and made it even more efficient. The Han era saw major developments in science, art, and literature.

In 220 CE the downfall of the Han was followed by nearly four centuries of unrest, known as the period of disunity. The empire split into three smaller kingdoms, and invaders from the north conquered northern China. In 581 CE the Sui dynasty reestablished imperial rule and began a new age of arts, architecture, and learning. Successive dynasties of emperors ruled China for another thirteen hundred years, until 1912, when the last emperor was deposed.

Food and Farming

Farming began in China more than eight thousand years ago. China is so big it has several different climates, and thus a variety of crops can be grown. In the cool, dry north, farmers grew wheat and millet. Flour from the grain was used to make dumplings and noodles. In warm, wet southern China rice has been the main crop and the staple food for over six thousand years. Later tea, hemp, and cotton were introduced.

As well as cereal crops, farmers grew vegetables and fruits such as pears and oranges. All over China people kept livestock, including oxen, pigs, ducks, chickens, and geese. For poor people meat, such as pork or horse, was a rare treat, tasted only on special occasions. Wealthy people enjoyed a much more varied diet,

▶ Rice was grown in flooded fields called paddies. This nineteenth-century painting shows Chinese farmers harvesting rice in the way it had been done for millennia.

including dishes made with lamb, duck, dog, and snake and flavored with spices.

In early times farmers used crude stone hoes and scythes to prepare the soil and reap the harvest. Iron-tipped ploughs pulled by oxen were in use by 600 BCE. During the Han dynasty the invention of many labor-saving devices eased the heavy work of farming. New inventions included the "endless wheel," an irrigation pump worked by human pedalers, and various grain-processing machines.

The Han emperor Wu Di (141–87 BCE) placed great emphasis on farming. He ordered large-scale public projects, such as canal digging. In practice his decrees meant that peasants were required to spend large amounts of time working on these irrigation projects instead of working in their own fields.

City Life

From early times the Chinese built great cities. Each dynasty tended to found a new capital from which the vast empire was ruled. Zengzhou was one of the first capitals, built by the Shang around 1600 BCE. The Qin emperor, Cheng, ruled from the city of Xianyang. The Han dynasty that replaced the Qin built a new capital at Chang'an.

Chang'an and other cities were laid out according to a grid plan, with streets running parallel and at right angles to one another. Towns were protected by high walls and sometimes moats with gates that were shut at dusk to keep intruders out. Every town held at least one busy market where traders sold their wares.

▲ This stone brick, from a tomb dating from the Han dynasty, shows a farmer plowing with an ox-drawn plow.

IN 111 BCE THE HAN EMPEROR WU DI DECLARED:

Agriculture is the basic occupation of the world. So the imperial government must cut canals and ditches, guide the rivers, and build reservoirs in order to prevent flood and drought.

▲ This painting shows the long, flowing robes worn by well-to-do Chinese scholars in ancient times.

farmers, who were highly valued for the food they produced though they were often poor. The third class was made up of craftsmen and other skilled workers. Merchants belonged to the lowest class, even though some of them were very rich.

Clothing was one way to tell rich people from poor. Noblemen and scholars wore fine silk robes dyed in rich colors and covered in embroidery. Only emperors were allowed to wear yellow silk. Poor people wore undyed cotton tunics and loose trousers. Peasants in the south wore cone-shaped hats for protection from the fierce sun. In the north jackets made from fleeces and furs were worn in cold weather.

Men and women were not equal in Chinese society. Marriage was the only career open to women, who could play no part in public life. During the Han dynasty noblewomen lived their whole lives behind the walls of their fine houses and rarely went outside. Poor peasant women living in the countryside were in some ways freer than the noblewomen, but the peasant women were burdened with work. They toiled in their fields and homes from morning until night.

Emperors and their staff, nobles, merchants, craftsmen, and poor people all lived in separate districts. Wealthy people lived in spacious dwellings with several courtyards and high walls that shut out the rest of the city. Poor people lived in cramped conditions in humble thatched huts.

Chinese Society

The Chinese saw society as being made up of four classes arranged in a hierarchy, one above the other. Everyone, from wealthy gentlemen to the poorest peasants, knew their place. The noblemen, scholars, and rich landowners were at the highest level, below the emperor. Beneath them were the

Trade and Transport

From around 200 BCE the first Chinese emperors began a program of constructing a network of roads to link distant parts of the empire. Only soldiers, officials, and the emperor's servants could use these good roads. Everyone else had to make their way along muddy tracks. Nobles and other wealthy people rode fine horses or traveled in chariots, carriages, or litters – chairs supported on long poles carried by two servants. Poorer people traveled mostly on foot and trundled their goods to market in ox-drawn carts.

CHINESE INVENTIONS

The ancient Chinese were skillful and inventive. Between the earliest times and 500 CE, they made many important discoveries and invented devices that are still in use. Around 1500 BCE Shang metal-workers learned to make bronze by melting copper and tin and mixing them together. They used this technique to make strong tools and weapons. By 600 BCE tools and weapons were made of an even stronger material, iron.

In the first century CE the Chinese invented the magnetic compass. They discovered that a magnetic iron needle would point north-south if floated in water on a sliver of wood. Early town-planners and architects used compasses to make sure that streets and houses faced in the right direction. Later, sailors used compasses to navigate at sea.

Wheelbarrows, another Chinese invention, date from around 100 CE. Farmers and traders used wheelbarrows to carry heavy loads to market, as well as to carry human passengers. Around 400 CE umbrellas were invented to protect people from rain and sunlight. They soon became popular throughout Asia.

▲ Part of the imperial fleet lies at anchor in a bay. This seventeenth-century silk painting shows the design of Chinese sailing ships in the sixth century CE..

▶ *This decorated bronze ax, dating from the Han dynasty, was used for ceremonial purposes only, not for war.*

From early times China's rivers and a network of artificial canals served as highways. Before about 1 CE most craft on the rivers were small wooden boats propelled by an oar or pole. During the Han dynasty rudders were fixed to the stern (rear) of boats to make them more maneuverable. This invention made it possible to build much larger ships.

Starting around two thousand years ago, silk became China's most valuable export. Over four thousand years ago, the Chinese had discovered how to weave this fine, soft fabric made from the cocoons of young silk moths. This skillful process was a carefully guarded secret in China and was kept from the outside world until the ninth century CE. During the Han era, caravans of camels loaded with bales of silk and other luxuries such as jade and spices made their way along trade routes that linked China with the west and Europe. The route became known as the Silk Road, after its most precious product.

War and Weapons

Many wars were fought throughout China's long history – some brief, others long and bloody. Soldiers of the Shang era fought in horse-drawn chariots using bronze weapons. By the third century BCE armies contained divisions of both mounted cavalry and foot-soldiers. Warriors of early imperial times were armed with iron weapons and protected by metal, leather, or quilted armour. They fought with swords, bows and arrows, crossbows, and halberds, which consisted of ax-like blades fixed to long poles.

Philosophy and Religion

In ancient China people followed three main religions or philosophies: Confucianism, Taoism, and Buddhism. They were known as the "three ways," and most people practiced elements of all three.

The Chinese worshiped hundreds of different gods, including the spirits of their ancestors and gods of natural features such as mountains and rivers. The principal god was Yu Huang Shang Di, the Jade Emperor. He ruled the earth and heavens through an army of lesser gods. The Jade Emperor's wife was Xi Wangmu, the Queen Mother of the West.

Literature and Learning

During the Shang era, around 3,500 years ago, the Chinese developed a system of writing. Early writings included songs, poems, prophecies, and lists of kings. The first records were scratched on animal bones or carved on stone. The invention of paper came much later, around 100 CE.

The scholars of ancient China studied many subjects, including philosophy, medicine, astronomy, and mathematics. A detailed chart of the heavens carved on a stone tablet has been found that dates back to 3000 BCE. Chinese interest in medicine dates back at least four thousand years. Early Chinese doctors knew that diet was important to health. To heal the sick, they used herbal medicines and acupuncture, which involves piercing the body with needles.

ZHANG HENG *78–139* CE

The inventor and philosopher Zhang Heng was a high-ranking civil servant during the late Han era. He excelled in many branches of science, being an expert mathematician and a skilled geographer. His most famous invention was the seismoscope, a machine for detecting earthquakes. It consisted of a large brass jar decorated with dragons' heads and containing a heavy pendulum. When a distant earthquake struck, the vibrations shook the jar and caused a ball to drop from one of the dragon's mouths into the mouth of a brass frog positioned below. In 138 CE Zhang Heng's seismoscope picked up vibrations from an earthquake 300 miles (483 km) away.

◀ This woodcut engraving shows Chinese women weaving silk on a large loom.

Chinese Philosophy

"Three ways flow into one" is an old Chinese saying. The three ways are the three main philosophies, or systems of thought, of ancient China: Confucianism, Taoism, and Buddhism. Taoism and Confucianism were founded in China. Buddhism is a religion that came originally from India. After the first century CE the three sets of ideas mingled in China, and many people followed elements of all three.

Confucianism, Taoism, and Buddhism all began at around the same time, in about 500 BCE. This period saw the dawn of a great age of philosophy in several civilizations, including China, India, and Greece. In China the sixth through third centuries BCE were a time of political unrest and social upheaval known as the Warring States period. At this time wars were frequent and crime was widespread. People turned to religion and philosophy for support.

Before 500 BCE the ancient Chinese had worshiped the spirits of natural forces such as the elements, rivers, and mountains. They carried out ceremonies to consult the ghosts of their ancestors when making important decisions in life. Around 500 BCE the new philosophies provided moral principles to replace some of the old superstitions and practices.

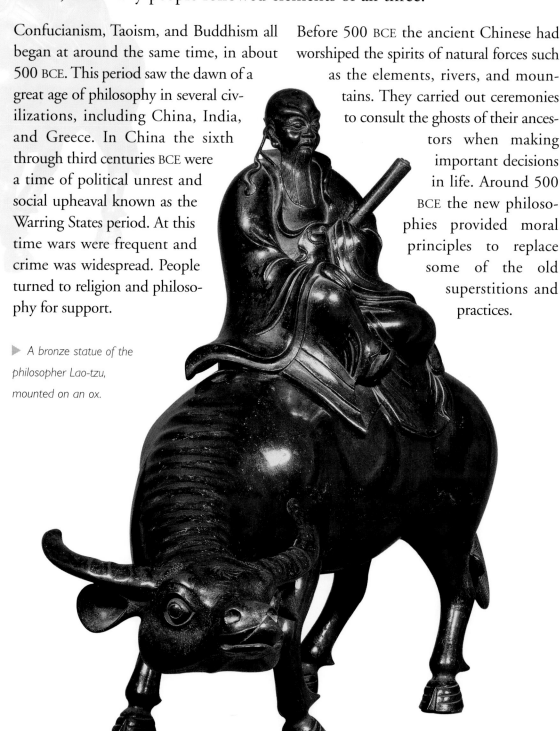

▶ A bronze statue of the philosopher Lao-tzu, mounted on an ox.

▲ *The philosopher Mencius helped Confucianism become a major philosophy in China.*

Confucianism

Confucianism was founded by the Chinese thinker Kong Qiu, who probably lived from 551 to 479 BCE. Kong Qiu was called Kong Fuzi (meaning Master Kong) by his followers, and is better known in the West by the Latin version of his name, Confucius.

Confucius was mainly concerned with ideas of morality – how people should live their lives and how rulers should govern. He stressed the importance of tradition, duty, and obedience. Young people should respect and obey their elders; wives should respect their husbands, and citizens their rulers. In turn, Confucius believed, rulers had a duty to their subjects to rule wisely and establish fair laws.

From the third century BCE to the third century CE, Confucianism was supported by the emperors of China and their officials because it encouraged people to respect and obey authority. Under the Han dynasty (206 BCE–220 CE) Confucianism became the official state philosophy, and the whole Chinese empire was run according to Confucian ideas and principles.

Taoism

Taoism (also spelled Daoism) is a religion as well as a philosophy. It is traditionally said to have been founded by a legendary thinker named Lao-tzu (also spelled Laozi), who according to legend was born in 604 BCE. He was a scholar who worked as a court librarian. Toward the end of his life, Lao-tzu mounted an ox and rode off in search of spiritual understanding and was never seen again. Lao-tzu was said to have written the first great work of Taoism, the *Tao Te Ching* (also spelled *Daodejing*). However, it is not certain that he really lived at all.

Taoism is a more spiritual philosophy than Confucianism. It is concerned with the Tao – the way of nature, the mysterious guiding force behind the universe. The Tao cannot be expressed in words; it must be experienced by its followers through inner understanding. Believers pray and meditate to achieve a sense of oneness with all things.

Taoists believe that two equal and opposite forces make up everything in the universe. They are yin and yang. Yin is cold, dark, moist, and feminine; yang is hot, light, dry, and masculine. Together they create balance and harmony. This principle is represented visually by a symbol made up of interlocking black and white forms. Since the founding of Taoism, its followers have tried to achieve harmony by balancing yin and yang in their daily lives.

Confucianism emphasizes duty and respect for law and order. In contrast, Taoists avoid social obligations and reject human-made laws. The early Taoists lived simple, spontaneous lives close to nature, filled with prayer and meditation. Later, during the Han dynasty, Taoism developed into a more complicated religion. It became mixed up with earlier folk beliefs and superstitions.

In the early centuries CE two different branches of Taoism developed. Both were concerned with the search for immortality (everlasting life). One branch was called the Cult of the Immortals. Followers worshiped eight supernatural beings who had become immortal. These beings had magical powers, such as the ability to become invisible, bring the dead to life, and turn things to gold. The other branch, known as the Way of the Heavenly Teacher, had many gods and ceremonies. Believers followed special diets and made offerings to the spirits in order to live longer lives.

Taoist beliefs are based on two main early sources, the *Tao Te Ching* and the *Chuang-tzu* (also spelled *Zhuangzi*). At least part of the *Chuang-tzu* is thought to have been written by the Taoist philosopher of the same name, who lived in the fourth century BCE. The *Chuang-tzu* is a great work of early Chinese literature, full of wit and lively insights. It urges its readers to seek harmony with nature by accepting and welcoming all natural processes, even death.

Buddhism

Buddhism, the third of China's three ways, began in India around 500 BCE. It was founded by a prince named Siddhartha Gautama (563–483 BCE), who is known as the Buddha, or Enlightened One. Around the age of thirty-five, Siddhartha succeeded in his quest to find the cause of suffering in the world. He realized that suffering was caused by people's ignorance and their

▼ *This nineteenth-century painting shows one of the eight Confucian Immortals playing a flute in Paradise.*

desire for earthly things. In reaching this understanding he entered a state of perfect peace, called nirvana. He spent the rest of his life trying to teach people how to achieve the same peace, by helping others and trying to live without desire.

In the centuries following Buddha's death, Buddhism spread through India to the island of Sri Lanka and Southeast Asia. It also spread northward to Tibet, and then east into China along the ancient trading route known as the Silk Road. Towns along the Silk Road, such as Dunhuang in northern China, became centers of Buddhist belief and art. Buddhism first reached China in the first century CE, but it did not become popular there until the third through sixth centuries CE. Like the period around 500 BCE that had seen the birth of Confucianism and Taoism, this was another time of war and upheaval, when people looked to religion for support.

ONE FAMOUS PASSAGE FROM THE *CHUANG-TZU* READS:

How do I know that hating death is not like having strayed from home when a child, and not knowing the way back?

SEE ALSO

- Analects • Buddha • Buddhism • China • Confucianism
- Dunhuang • Lao-tzu

Christianity

Christianity is a religion based on the life and teachings of Jesus of Nazareth. Christians believe that Jesus was God in human form. Before the birth of Jesus, Jews had long believed that God would send a messiah (a word that means "anointed of God") and that the messiah would create a kingdom of heaven on earth for all Jews.

When Jesus was crucified, he said he was dying for all mankind. According to the New Testament of the Bible, three days later he came back to life and spoke to his followers again and then ascended to heaven. After witnessing this miracle, Jesus' followers proclaimed him Christ (a word that means the same as *messiah*). They were the first Christians. The religion they preached is now the largest in the world.

After Jesus' death Christianity spread quickly outward from Palestine. Communities of Christians expected that soon – perhaps within their lifetime – history would end and Jesus would return again and create a kingdom not just for Jews but for anyone in the whole world who became a Christian.

A great number of Christians were killed by the Roman government for their beliefs. However, in 312 CE Emperor Constantine converted to Christianity, and in 381 Emperor Theodosius made it the official religion of the Roman Empire. By 500 one in four people in the known world were Christian.

The Apostolic Churches

As Jesus preached, told stories, and healed people, he was accompanied by twelve men, called apostles. Jesus gave them a mission to pass on the message that he had

▶ A sixth-century mosaic of the Last Supper. Jesus broke some bread and shared it with the disciples, and then passed round the wine. This ceremony, called the Eucharist, is carried out by Christians all over the world. The mosaic is in Sant'Apollinare in Ravenna, Italy.

THE NEW TESTAMENT

The Bible, the sacred book of the Christian religion, is divided into two parts, which Christians call the Old Testament and the New Testament. The New Testament contains twenty-seven books by about ten different writers. It was written largely in Greek between 50 and 150 CE. It contains four Gospels, different versions of the life and death of Jesus. It tells of his followers, relates the struggles of the early Church, and gives advice on how to be a good Christian. It concludes with a vision of the end of the world.

taught them. After his death, they spread themselves throughout the Roman Empire. People came in the thousands to hear them preach. These communities of Christians were the first churches. The twelve were joined by Paul, whose letters of advice, written to all the new churches he visited, are part of the New Testament. Each church was headed by a bishop, appointed to succeed the apostles after their death.

Christian Writers

In the first centuries after Jesus' death, the Bible was copied by hand and translated into many European and Asian languages. The message of Christianity was also spread by some outstanding writers. Clement of Alexandria and his pupil, Origen, combined the teachings of Jesus with some popular aspects of Greek philosophy to increase the appeal of Christianity to the Greeks. Augustine's ideas and interpreta-

tions of the Bible were extremely influential. In about 400 CE Jerome translated the entire Bible into Latin for the first time.

Persecution

Early Christians were considered by Jews and Romans to be detached from the world. Their beliefs did not allow them to join the army, read classical poetry, or go to the theater. Although they did charitable work, the Christians were very unpopular with the Roman government.

▲ This is an underground cemetery in Rome, known as the Catacombs of Calixtus. About half a million Christians, including nine third-century popes, were buried here. Rome has six hundred miles (960 km) of catacombs.

Whenever a disaster occurred, the Romans believed it was a sign their gods were angry. Often they blamed Christians and killed them. After a terrible fire in Rome in 64 CE, the emperor, Nero, set fire to Christians and used them as human torches in his gardens.

In many ways the persecutions suffered by Christians helped Christianity to become stronger. A person who dies for his or her faith is known as a martyr, and as the writer Tertullian said in about 200 CE, "the blood of the marytrs is the seed of the church." By 500 there were over two and a half million martyrs.

After Constantine

The fourth century CE saw a huge growth in Christianity. In 313 Emperor Constantine legalized Christianity. The Christian community became very large, and disagreements emerged, especially about how it was possible for Jesus to be human and divine at the same time. It became necessary to decide upon some standard principles and forms of Christian worship and belief.

Three great councils were held at Nicaea (in 325), at Constantinople (in 381), and at Chalcedon (in 451), all in modern-day Turkey. Bishops came from throughout the Roman Empire to debate and vote, and the decisions they made are still in force. In 367 Athanasius, bishop of Alexandria, chose the books that would be included in the official New Testament. Constantine ordered the building of the first great churches, often on the sites of pagan temples. The Christian Church started to organize itself into a hierarchy. The five most important bishops were the patriarchs of Antioch, Alexandria, Constantinople, and Jerusalem and the pope, the bishop of Rome. Local bishops became powerful and respected figures in society.

By the end of the fourth century, Christianity was the official religion of the Roman Empire. The new churches were full, and the services started to have a more uniform look and sound, with psalms, readings, and sermons. After four hundred years of persecution, the Christian Church itself started persecuting nonbelievers.

▼ *This seventeenth-century fresco of the Council of Nicaea can be found in a library in Vatican City, the administrative center of the Roman Catholic Church. The decisions made by the bishops at Nicaea remain in force. It was here that the method of dating the festival of Easter was established.*

Key Beliefs and Practices

Christianity is a monotheistic religion; that is to say, Christians believe there is only one God. They believe that God is a Trinity, a word meaning "three in one." As the Father he is the creator of the world who watches over people and will judge them at the end of time. As the Son he is Jesus Christ, who became human to save people from sin. As the Holy Spirit he sanctifies the natural world, residing in people's hearts, homes, and churches.

PETER

"Follow me and I will make you fishers of men." A man called Simon was fishing one day when Jesus walked up and spoke these words. Simon threw aside his net and became Jesus' leading apostle. Jesus changed Simon's name to Peter, from the Latin for "rock." Jesus wanted Peter to be the rock on which the Christian Church would be built. Peter was impulsive and full of love for Jesus. When soldiers came to arrest Jesus, Peter was furious and, lashing out with his sword, cut one soldier's ear off. He learned from his mistakes, and Jesus made him leader of the Twelve. Christians traditionally regard him as the first pope. It is believed that he was executed and buried in Rome in 64 CE.

◀ This mosaic of St Peter dates from around 700 CE. It can be found in a crypt of St Peter's Church in Vatican City, Rome, one of the world's most famous churches.

Christians believe that God made the world for the sake of love, and Christians show they love God in return by worshiping him in hymns and prayers and living according to the teachings of Jesus. The most important act of worship is the Eucharist, or Holy Communion, when Christians take bread and wine in memory of Jesus. The most important Christian symbol is the cross. For Christians the cross marks the greatest moment in human history. When he was crucified, Jesus said he was suffering punishment for all the sins of mankind. Because of this sacrifice Christians believe they will enjoy salvation, that is, after death they will be resurrected and live forever with God in heaven.

Conclusion

Christianity now comprises hundreds of different churches, all with different customs, beliefs, and practices. It is more than a system of beliefs. For hundreds of millions of people, Christianity is a complete way of life. It has inspired great works of art, poetry, music, and architecture. Many wars have been fought in its name. However, at its heart remains Jesus' simple message: "Love God, love your neighbors, love your enemies."

◀ This manuscript of the four Gospels dates from around 1100 CE. It is held at the National Gallery of Victoria in Melbourne, Australia.

SEE ALSO
- Constantine • Jerusalem
- Jesus of Nazareth • Judaism
- Nero • Paul of Tarsus • Religion
- Roman Republic and Empire

Cicero

Marcus Tullius Cicero (106–43 BCE) was an important figure in the Roman Republic. He was a famous writer and politician who took part in the struggle for power that went on in Rome following the death of Julius Caesar, and he was eventually destroyed by his own attempts to influence events. He is best remembered for his writing, which is considered the high point of Latin prose style.

His Life

Cicero was from a wealthy Roman family. He held several senior positions in the Roman government and was elected consul (one of two very powerful magistrates) in 63 BCE. In the same year he prevented a group of aristocrats, led by Catiline, from trying to seize power, and he carried out the will of the Roman senate by ordering the execution of five of them. As a result, he was hailed as "father of his country."

Five years later, when the senate was no longer worried about conspirators, Cicero was banished from Rome because he had executed the five men without a trial. In 57 BCE, he persuaded several leading senators to support him and returned to Rome. For a few years he supported the men in power – Pompey, Caesar, and Crassus – but around 55 BCE he virtually gave up public life and began to concentrate on writing.

In 52 Cicero was persuaded to take up another government post, this time as governor of the province of Cilicia in Asia Minor, where he put down a rebellion. He was rewarded with a small ceremony in his honor in which the city gave thanks for his work. Cicero, who had hoped to receive a triumphal procession through Rome with much music and feasting, was disappointed.

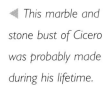

◄ This marble and stone bust of Cicero was probably made during his lifetime.

When Cicero returned to Rome in 49 BCE, Caesar and Pompey, the two joint rulers, had fallen out, and Caesar had established himself as dictator in Rome. Cicero again retired to his writing and took no part in the assassination of Caesar in 44. Afterward he tried to use Caesar's adopted son, Octavian (later known as Augustus), to seek power in Rome. When Octavian took power himself, he pursued Cicero and had him killed. Cicero's head and hands were put on display at the speaker's stand in the Roman senate.

His Works

During his lifetime Cicero was best known as a politician, and his skill as an orator (a public speaker) made him very famous. He published many of his speeches to the senate, as well as letters to his allies and friends. His longer works were written before he became governor of Cilicia and after Caesar became dictator. He wrote on political topics, such as the importance of the republican state, law, and human rights, and about ethics, philosophy, and theology. He also wrote some poetry and books about how to make good speeches.

CATILINE c.108–62 BCE

Lucius Sergius Catilina came from a noble family. Like Cicero, he worked hard to achieve power in the Roman senate. However, rumors of misconduct, including accusations of murder, held back his political career. Frustrated with his failure to become consul, he conspired to overthrow the Roman Republic and sieze power for himself with the help of a group of dissatisfied Roman citizens. Cicero heard of the conspiracy and arrested some of them. Catiline fled to Etruria, and an army was sent after him. He and all his followers died in the ensuing battle. Catiline's death made Cicero a popular man.

SEE ALSO
- Augustus • Caesar, Julius
- Roman Republic and Empire

Cities

In ancient times, cities grew up in many parts of the world, including Asia, Europe, Africa, and Central America. The size, scale, and organization of ancient cities varied, but all were busy centers, crowded with people going about their daily lives.

The First Settlements

In prehistoric times the first humans lived as nomadic wanderers. They moved from place to place as they hunted animals and gathered wild foods. During the Neolithic period (New Stone Age), around ten thousand years ago, people began to settle in one place and build permanent dwellings. Archaeologists believe that this great change came about because of the development of farming.

Around 8000 BCE humans first learned to regulate the flow of water by digging channels to irrigate fields. Following this breakthrough, farmers began to raise crops and domesticate animals. The first settlements sprang up; later they grew into towns and cities.

As farming practices became more efficient, a surplus of food was produced. People were able to leave the work of farming and find other jobs. Some became craft workers such as potters and weavers; others became miners or toolmakers. The first cities were home to these nonfarmers, who made a living by trading the things they produced for food in public markets.

The First Towns and Cities

Jericho in Palestine is the site of the oldest town so far discovered. The ruins there date back ten thousand years to 8000 BCE. Ancient Jericho was fortified with stout stone walls and had a tall watchtower. Jericho's citizens traded with other parts of western Asia.

◀ Part of the moat and walls of the ancient city of Jericho. Finds such as cowrie shells from the Red Sea show that Jericho was an important trading center.

▲ The Indus valley in northern India was home to a great civilization by 2500 BCE. The city of Mohenjo Daro held fine buildings and well-paved streets.

stone obsidian, which was used to make sharp tools. The stone was probably a major source of wealth for Çatal Hüyük.

In other regions cities also grew up close to valuable natural resources such as forests or minerals. A good source of water nearby was essential to the growth of all cities. A river or lake might also make a city easier to defend. As a city developed, being near a river or on a coastline also aided transport and communication.

The First Great Cities

The world's first great cities developed in the land of Sumer in Mesopotamia around 4500 BCE. Cities also developed in other parts of the world. In the Nile valley in Egypt, towns existed by at least 3500 BCE. In the Indus valley in northwest India, cities first appeared around 2500 BCE. In China the first cities were probably built around 1600 BCE, while in Central America they date from 200 BCE.

Features of Cities

A good defensive position was very important for an ancient city. Rome and Athens were founded on hills where people could retreat in times of danger. Most cities had stout defensive walls and sometimes a moat. Many included a citadel, which was a fortress built on high ground.

As well as private houses, most cities had public spaces that were used as markets. Public buildings included temples, warehouses for storing food, and sometimes communal baths. Temples and royal palaces, such as those in ancient Greece and China, occupied considerable space in cities. In Mesopotamian cities, such as Babylon, a high temple mound called a ziggurat occupied up to a third of the space inside the city walls.

The town of Çatal Hüyük, located in present-day Turkey, is another very early settlement, dating to around 6700 BCE. On the nearby plain archaeologists have discovered remains of irrigation channels – evidence that farming was taking place. Hills near the town contained the hard volcanic

Government

The earliest cities were mostly ruled by priests. Later, nonreligious rulers such as kings and emperors took over the task of government. They appointed officials to enforce the law and to collect taxes, which funded the costs of administration and the construction of buildings such as temples and palaces. In some areas, for example, in ancient Greece, the cities were independent of any higher authority. These city-states ruled over the surrounding region.

Health and Sanitation

In many ancient cities sanitation was a problem. Citizens threw rubbish and other waste from their houses onto the streets, where it collected, or piled it high by the city walls. In such conditions disease spread quickly. However, some ancient cities had good sanitation. Rome had a well-planned sewer system and public baths, and water supplies entered the city by way of aqueducts.

In the days of the Roman Empire, Roman cities were noisy, bustling places. The Roman writer Juvenal (c. 60–140 CE) marveled how anyone could rest:

The noise of carts thundering along the narrow streets and the language of the drivers when they get stuck in a traffic jam would wake even the heaviest sleeper.

SEE ALSO

▼ *The city of Rome included an open area called the Forum where people could gather. The Basilica (church) of Constantine, shown here, was built in the Forum around 300 CE.*

Claudius

Claudius (10 BCE–54 CE) was an unlikely choice for emperor. He was fifty when he became ruler of the Roman Empire. Until the emperor Caligula made him a senator and consul in 37 CE, Claudius had led a reclusive life. He had a speech impediment and tended to dribble, and his family assumed he was mentally backward. In fact, he was an extremely intelligent man and proved to be a good emperor.

The Unlikely Emperor

The murder of Caligula plunged Rome into chaos. The Roman senate wanted to restore the Republic, while the soldiers of the praetorian guard needed a new emperor to assure their own position of power as his protectors. As Caligula's uncle, Claudius was viewed as a possible successor. The praetorians therefore proclaimed Claudius emperor on the day of Caligula's assassination, in late January 41 CE.

A marble bust of Claudius dating from the first century CE. The sculptor has been careful to flatter the emperor by improving on his looks.

Like Caligula, Claudius lived in constant fear of assassination. He rapidly tried to repair the damage done by his nephew by issuing pardons and returning confiscated lands and property. Unlike Caligula, he was aware that a degree of popularity went a long way toward ensuring his own survival and a lengthy reign. On the other hand, Claudius also ordered the death of some three hundred noblemen and thirty-five senators during his reign because he suspected them of plotting against him.

Consolidation

Claudius made a point of treating the senate with respect. He took an interest in justice and finance and courted popularity among the people by promoting public games. He also ordered a wide-ranging building program, which included two new aqueducts, two new roads, and a new harbor at the Roman port of Ostia.

Conquest and Betrayal

Claudius seemed an unlikely military commander. However, in 43 CE, to help win the favor of the nobility in Rome, he ordered an invasion of Britain. Aided by his general Aulus Plautius, he succeeded in conquering the island where Julius Caesar and Caligula had failed. This success did a great deal to boost his popularity, both among the ruling classes and the people.

In 49 Claudius was persuaded to marry for the fourth time. His new wife, Agrippina, was Caligula's younger sister and Claudius's niece. She schemed to ensure that her son from a previous marriage would succeed Claudius as emperor – not Claudius's son Britannicus. She succeeded, and Claudius named her son, Lucius Domitius Ahenobarbus (more commonly known as Nero), joint inheritor along with Britannicus. Nero, being older, became more likely to succeed to the imperial throne.

Only Claudius himself now stood in Agrippina's way. It is possible that she arranged for his food (a special mushroom dish) to be poisoned. Claudius died on October 13, 54, and was declared a god. Nero was later rumored to have declared mushrooms to be the food of the gods, "since Claudius, by means of the mushroom, became one."

Legacy

Claudius's reign brought stability to the Roman Empire as a whole. He worked hard for the welfare of his subjects. His administrative reforms survived the erratic reign of his successor, Nero, and may have helped preserve the empire itself in future years.

▲ This drawing of the port of Ostia was made in the sixteenth century and shows Claudius's semicircular harbor on the right. The hexagonal harbor on the left was built by the emperor Trajan more than fifty years later.

THE FOLLOWING IS A DESCRIPTION OF THE MOMENT WHEN CLAUDIUS DISCOVERED HE WAS EMPEROR.

In great terror at the news of the murder, he stole away to a balcony and hid among the curtains. … As he cowered there, a common soldier saw his feet and pulled him out and recognized him; and when Claudius fell at his feet in terror, he hailed him as emperor.

SUETONIUS, *LIFE OF CLAUDIUS*

SEE ALSO

- Aqueducts • Caesar, Julius • Caligula • Nero
- Roman Republic and Empire

Cleopatra

Cleopatra (c.69–30 BCE) was pharaoh of Egypt from 51 BCE to 30 BCE. She was the last person to rule Egypt before it was absorbed by the Roman Empire.

Ruling Egypt

Cleopatra was the daughter of the pharaoh Ptolemy XII and began to rule Egypt at about age eighteen. At first Cleopatra ruled with her father. When he died, in 50 BCE, she ruled with her brother, Ptolemy XIII.

Ptolemy XIII was about seven years younger than Cleopatra. He did not want to share power with her, and in 48 BCE Cleopatra discovered he was plotting to kill her so that he could rule Egypt alone. Cleopatra fled and set about raising an army to defeat her brother. The most

▶ Fragment of a relief, believed to be a portrait of Queen Cleopatra. Traces of a grid can be seen, indicating that it is either unfinished or was used by sculptors as a model.

powerful army in the world was the Roman army, which had already helped her father keep power in Egypt. Cleopatra asked the Roman general Julius Caesar for help.

Julius Caesar

Caesar was glad to help. The Romans already had a hold on Egypt, and helping Cleopatra would make this hold stronger. However, many people in Alexandria, Egypt's capital city, supported Ptolemy. The fighting continued until 47 BCE, when the Roman army put Cleopatra back in power, this time ruling with her ten-year-old brother, Ptolemy XIV.

In June 47 BCE Cleopatra had a baby, Caesar's son, named Caesarion. The following year Caesar was back in Rome, and Cleopatra joined him there. Just two years later, in 44, he was assassinated, and Cleopatra returned to Egypt.

Mark Antony

Soon afterward Ptolemy XIV died, possibly killed on Cleopatra's orders, and Cleopatra ruled Egypt with Caesarion. The people of Alexandria were even less happy with Cleopatra after she had deserted Egypt for Rome and possibly murdered her brother, so she still needed Roman help to stay in power. The Romans had their own problems: Octavian, Julius Caesar's great-nephew, and the general Mark Antony were locked in a power struggle.

Mark Antony helped Cleopatra stay in power, and he lived with her in her palace at Alexandria. In 40 BCE Cleopatra and Mark Antony's twins, Cleopatra and Alexander, were born, but by this time Mark Antony was back in Rome. He had made peace with Octavian and married Octavian's sister.

In 37 BCE Mark Antony returned to Egypt – he and Octavian were enemies again. By 35 he and Cleopatra had another son, Ptolemy. However, relations with Octavian were so bad that in 32 Octavian persuaded the Roman senate to go to war with Cleopatra. The war went on until 30 BCE. In August of that year, Octavian defeated Antony and Cleopatra's armies, and Antony killed himself.

Death

Octavian's victorious army marched into Alexandria. Cleopatra had fought with Antony against Octavian, and she knew Octavian would not let her live, so Cleopatra killed herself. Caesarion had already been caught and executed. Octavian took over Egypt for Rome.

◀ This Roman coin was issued to celebrate the defeat of Antony and Cleopatra in 30 BCE. It shows a crocodile, which Romans would instantly associate with Egypt, and the words Aegypt capta, meaning "Egypt captured."

SEE ALSO

Clothes

Long before humans started wearing clothes, they decorated their bodies with charms and ornaments, including shells, bones, flowers, and pebbles. The Neanderthals (primitive relatives of humans) captured wild animals and used their skins to make loincloths and other simple garments. At first they clipped the hides together with fish bones, thorns, or flints. Later they learned to make strong thread from the guts of slain animals.

▼ This decoration on a casket from around 1330 BCE shows King Tutankhamen and his queen Ankhesenamen. Their costumes and jewelry are clearly shown. The queen is wearing the fine, flowing, linen robes typical of royalty during this period.

Leather

Rawhide was uncomfortable to wear and fell apart quickly; early humans tried to find ways of softening it and making it last. By 20,000 BCE they were drying animal skins in the hot sun. Oil and animal fat were rubbed into the hides to make them soft and pliable. Some early hunters preserved the skins by salting them; others used smoke.

Woolen Clothes

The Mesopotamians started domesticating sheep around 9000 BCE. They used the wool to make comfortable and long-lasting garments. At first they used to roll the wool by hand – a lengthy process. However, by 7000 BCE they were using spindles.

The early Sumerians wore sheepskin skirts with the wool combed into tufts for decoration. This early form of kilt was kept in place with pins and reached to just below the knees. By 2500 BCE the sheepskin was replaced by proper woven wool. Long cloaks came into fashion, complemented by elaborate hairstyles, headdresses, and gold jewelry inlaid with semiprecious stones.

Linen

The Egyptians started making linen in the Neolithic period (c. 8000–5000 BCE). They harvested flax plants from the banks of the Nile and soaked them in water before extracting the fibers, which they beat and spun into cloth. Strong yet cool to wear, linen was the perfect material for the hot North African climate. The Egyptians considered linen a sacred material, believing that the gods themselves wore linen.

Egyptian clothes were loose pieces of cloth draped around the body with very little stitching. They were held in place with sashes or belts. The men wore simple linen skirts that were often pleated. The rich

COSMETICS

The Egyptians were using cosmetics by at least 4000 BCE. Makeup implements have been found in their tombs. Both men and women outlined their eyes with kohl and painted their fingernails and toenails with henna, a reddish-brown dye. Women rouged their cheeks. Wigs were worn to protect the head from the sun and reduce the risk of head lice.

In Babylon men curled their long hair and beards and used perfume and oil to give their hair a luxurious shine. Greek men also wore their hair long and perfumed. Some used bleach in order to appear blond.

Fashionable Roman girls powdered their faces to make them look pale. They also applied false beauty spots. Lipstick, often made from ficus or crushed shells, was applied daily. Vain Roman men wore wigs to hide bald patches. In certain eras the most popular wigs were those made from the hair of foreign slaves.

◀ These three items are from Mohenjo Daro, India. A lady would hold the hand mirror (top) while applying eye ointment with the rounded stick shown resting in a small pot for makeup (bottom left). The third item is a copper hairpin.

decorated their belts with pendants. Women wore long, narrow dresses that reached from their chest to their ankles, held in place with shoulder straps. These garments developed in time into more flowing robes.

Cotton

The people of the Indus valley in India were weaving cotton as early as 3000 BCE. In the cities of Mohenjo-Daro and Harappa people used spindles to weave cotton and wool. The materials were used to make both long shawls that men wore around their shoulders and cotton skirts and girdles for women.

This first-century-CE fresco shows a fashionable Roman lady pouring perfume into a vial. Perfume was very popular with Roman women. They kept it in small glass bottles or tiny onyx decanters.

THE GREEK HISTORIAN HERODOTUS DESCRIBES COTTON PLANTS HE SAW DURING A TRIP TO INDIA AROUND 430 BCE:

There are trees which grow wild there, the fruit wherof is a wool exceeding in beauty and goodness that of sheep. The natives make their clothes of this tree wool.

Both sexes complemented their clothes with jewelry – amulets for the men and bracelets and necklaces for the women. Indian cotton was of such good quality that by 63 BCE it was being exported to Europe, where it was used for clothing by rich citizens of the Roman Empire.

Roman Clothes

The early Romans copied their simple style of dress from the Greeks. However, as their empire grew in size and power, Romans started to wear more elaborate clothing, using materials and styles from all around the empire. As in other cultures, clothes in ancient Rome were worn as symbols of wealth, power, and social standing.

Togas – huge, semicircular pieces of woollen material wrapped around the body – could be worn only by male citizens. All men were allowed to wear a tunica, a simple garment copied from the short Greek tunic called a chiton, but only upper-class citizens were allowed to wear it in white. The lower classes had to be content with brown. Purple-dyed cloth was reserved for the extremely rich and the emperor.

With the advent of Christianity around 60 CE, a new style of dress began to be favored. Many early Christians rejected revealing clothes in favor of humbler wear designed to hide the body. As Christianity spread, the custom grew and was adopted throughout the Western world.

SEE ALSO

- Babylonians • Christianity • Egypt
- Greece, Classical • Indus Valley
- Mesopotamia
- Roman Republic and Empire
- Social Hierarchy • Sumer

Colosseum

The Colosseum in Rome, Italy, is one of the most famous of all Roman buildings. A vast, oval-shaped, open-air amphitheater, it was used for over four hundred years and has been described as the Eighth Wonder of the Ancient World. Romans flocked to this arena to watch games where people and animals were put to death in the name of public entertainment.

Building the Colosseum

The identity of the person who designed the Colosseum is not known. It was begun during the reign of Emperor Vespasian (reigned 69–79 CE), replacing an earlier amphitheater made of wood. The Colosseum took around ten years to build and was constructed from various forms of stone: travertine, marble, concrete, and tufa. An estimated 292,000 cartloads of stone were needed just to build its outside wall.

When finished, it could seat at least 45,000 people, with room for a further five thousand standing spectators. Crowd control was an important part of the building's design. Around the outside, at ground level, were eighty entrances (*vomitoria*) that led to corridors and staircases. With so many openings the public went to and from their seats quickly and easily. On hot days a sunshade (*velarium*) was extended over the spectators to keep them cool and comfortable.

Games at the Colosseum

Most Romans liked blood sports, and the Colosseum was designed as the stadium in which to stage them. From the day it opened in 80 CE, it was little more than a killing ground. Games at the Colosseum followed a set pattern. The day started with animal hunts (*venationes*). The mood changed at midday when criminals were executed.

▼ *The Roman name for the Colosseum was the Flavian Amphitheater, or simply the Amphitheater. It became known as the Colosseum only in the 700s CE, the name coming from a gigantic statue, or colosseus, of Emperor Nero (reigned 54–68 CE), which stood near to it.*

In the afternoon came the highlight of the games – contests between professional fighters, called gladiators, in which armed men, and occasionally women, fought to please the crowd. Their fights usually ended in the death of one of the fighters, although if they both fought well, their lives could be spared.

Last Days of the Colosseum

In 326 CE, during the reign of Rome's first Christian emperor, Constantine, gladiatorial games at the Colosseum were stopped. Constantine and many other Romans regarded them as barbaric, pagan acts. However, not all Romans agreed. Attempts were made to revive gladiator contests at the Colosseum, and the last known fight took place there in 404 CE, after which Emperor Honorius (reigned 395–423 CE) banned them once and for all. However, the Colosseum continued to be used for animal hunts for about another two hundred years. Afterwards it was used in turn as a small Christian cemetery, a fortress, and finally a quarry. Its marble was ripped up and burned to make lime or used to construct new buildings in Rome.

HERE IS A DESCRIPTION OF THE OPENING GAMES AT THE COLOSSEUM:

There was a battle between cranes and also between four elephants; animals both tame and wild were slain to the number of nine thousand; and women took part in dispatching them. As for the men, several fought in single combat and several groups contended together, both in infantry and naval battles. The arena suddenly filled with water, and people in ships engaged in a sea fight there. These were the spectaculars that were offered, and they continued for one hundred days.

DIO CASSIUS, HISTORY OF ROME, BOOK 66

▼ A mosaic of two heavily armed and armored gladiators, fighting with short swords. Between them stands the referee. His job was to see that the fighters fought well and did not fake their duel. If a man lost a piece of armor, the referee could stop the fight while the gladiator put it back on.

SEE ALSO

- Architecture • Constantine
- Roman Republic and Empire
- Rome, City of
- Sports and Entertainment

Confucianism

Confucianism is a philosophy based on the teachings of the Chinese thinker Confucius, who lived around 500 BCE. Confucius has been called the "uncrowned emperor of China" because his ideas were so influential. From around 200 BCE to 500 CE and for many centuries afterward, Confucian ideas formed the basis of the Chinese system of government and, indeed, influenced every aspect of Chinese life.

Confucianism is not a religion; it has no gods or priests and is not concerned with the idea of life after death. The teachings of Confucius are more a system of thought, offering guidance for just government and good personal behavior.

A Lost Golden Age

Confucius lived during a time of unrest in China, the period when the reign of a long line of kings called the Zhou was ending. The Zhou's control over China had weakened. Powerful lords were rebelling against their authority and fighting one another, and there was constant war. Confucius looked back to the early days of the Zhou dynasty, around 1000 BCE, when he believed society had been more orderly and peaceful. He longed for this lost golden age of justice and tranquillity to return.

Confucian Ideas

Confucius's ideas are summed up in a book called the *Analects*, or *Conversations*.

Confucius stressed the importance of respect, duty, and obedience in both public and private life. He taught that children should respect and obey their parents, and wives should respect their husbands. Well-ordered family life was central to Confucian thinking. Confucius encouraged the practice of ancestor worship because he believed it would strengthen family ties.

▼ This eighteenth-century Korean print shows students in a classroom learning the principles of Confucian thought.

As well as urging order and obedience in family life, Confucius stressed that all citizens should respect and obey their ruler. In turn, rulers should rule wisely and respect the gods. Powerful men should lead by example, not act harshly and tyrannically. Confucius believed it was more important for rulers to set a good example than to pass harsh laws. If everyone, from rich noblemen to poor people, lived dutifully and honestly, then society would be transformed from top to bottom. The prosperous, just society of the golden age would return.

Confucianism Takes Hold

Confucius's ideas did not become popular in his lifetime. The philosopher worked as a minor government official and died almost unknown in 479 BCE. After Confucius's death his ideas were developed and made famous by his disciples, including Mencius (c. 390–305 BCE) and Xunzi (315–236 BCE). They believed that, if everyone lived by these rules, peace and justice would follow naturally. One of Confucius's most important sayings is known as the golden rule: "Do not do to others what you would not want done to yourself."

During the fourth and third centuries BCE, war and unrest continued in China as the power of the Zhou disintegrated still further. This age of Chinese history is known as the Warring States period. Around 220 BCE a powerful prince named Cheng (c. 259–210 BCE), head of a people called the Qin, succeeded in defeating his

▼ The temple complex of Confucius at Qufu in Shandong Province, eastern China. Shandong was the philosopher's home province.

▲ This nineteenth-century illustration shows the Chinese philosopher Confucius instructing his disciples.

rivals and became the first emperor of a united China.

Cheng was a harsh emperor who inspired fear rather than love in his people. He thoroughly rejected Confucian ideals on moral behavior and is believed to have buried some of Confucius's followers alive. He certainly banned all their books. Soon after Cheng's death another dynasty, the Han, seized the throne and ruled China for the next four centuries. The Han emperors restored Confucianism and promoted it as the official belief system, and it retained this status right up to the beginning of the twentieth century.

Confucius and the Civil Service

Han emperors embraced and further developed the system of strong, centralized government that Cheng had established. The

CONFUCIUS c.551–479 BCE

In 551 BCE Confucius was born with the name Kong Qiu in the state of Lu, in a region now part of Shandong Province in eastern China. The name Confucius, which is a Latin version of Kong Fuzi, the title given him by his followers, means "great master Kong." Although Confucius was young when his father died, Confucius received a good education. When he grew up, he became a scholar and developed his ideas on just government and moral behavior. As an adult Confucius sought the chance to put his ideas into practice. He applied for a key post as adviser to a ruler but failed to get it. Thereafter he held a series of minor government posts until the age of fifty. Around 500 BCE Confucius left his job and traveled around China. He moved from state to state, giving rulers advice on how to govern their lands. Around 487 BCE he returned to his home state and spent the rest of his life teaching and editing works of classical literature. He is thought to have died in 479 BCE at the age of seventy-two.

Han empire was run by a civil service made up of thousands of officials, each in charge of a small area, who reported to their superiors in the hierarchy. The chief ministers answered to the emperor himself.

The civil service was designed and run according to Confucian principles. In 124 BCE the Han emperor Wu Di established a university where certain highly recommended young men were sent to study Confucian thought. The university curriculum focused on the five books of Confucian ideas that were known as the Five Classics. In order to obtain a position in the civil service, students had to learn these works by heart and then take examinations that tested their grasp of the principles of Confucianism.

Several centuries later the opportunity to take these examinations was opened to nearly all Chinese men who wished to follow a career as a government official. High-ranking civil service jobs would be open to those who passed. Success in getting such a job would probably also assure marriage into a wealthy family. Some students were so desperate to pass the examination that they resorted to cheating, but there were stern punishments for anyone caught doing so.

Confucius had believed that education was important for everyone, not just wealthy and privileged people. In practice, however, almost all students came from the ruling class of noble families. For over two thousand years, from the mid-100s BCE until the early 1900s CE, China was run by an elite of Confucian scholars. No other civilization before or since has placed so much importance on philosophy.

▶ *Candidates for the Chinese civil service sit for an examination in Confucian philosophy.*

SEE ALSO
- Analects • Cheng • China
- Chinese Philosophy

CONFUCIUS'S BELIEF THAT SOCIETY WILL RUN SMOOTHLY IF EVERYONE KNOWS HIS OR HER PLACE IS SUMMED UP IN THE FOLLOWING SAYING:

Let the prince be a prince, the minister a minister, the father a father, and the son a son.

Constantine

Constantine (c. 272–337 CE) has been called the most important emperor of the later Roman Empire. Under his rule Christianity became the official religion of the Romans, and he moved the capital away from Rome to a new city in the east, Byzantium.

The Later Roman Empire

The power of the Romans declined during the third century CE. The empire was weakened by outbreaks of famine and divided by civil wars, and its frontiers were frequently breached by barbarians. It became difficult to keep the Roman Empire together, and for this reason it was split into an eastern and a western part, each with its own emperor.

In 306 CE two men were proclaimed emperors of the Western Empire – Constantine and his rival Maxentius. Each wanted to rule as sole emperor. Civil war broke out, and on October 28, 312, the armies of Constantine and Maxentius clashed at the Milvian Bridge, a crossing over the Tiber River, north of Rome. Constantine was victorious and became sole emperor of the Western Empire.

Constantine and Christianity

Shortly before the battle of the Milvian Bridge, Constantine had a vision. He saw a cross of light shining in the sky. On it was written a prophecy that said he would be the victor in the approaching battle. The next night Christ appeared to Constantine and told him to place the sign of the cross at the head of his army as he went into battle. Constantine believed that the God of the Christians had helped him defeat Maxentius.

Early the following year, 313, Constantine issued a proclamation stating that Christian worship would be tolerated throughout the Roman Empire. Known as the Edict of Milan, it allowed Christians to openly worship their God without fear of persecution. Within seventy years Christianity had become the state religion of the empire, and the worship of the old pagan gods slowly ceased.

▼ Constantine the Great, shown on a gold coin known as a solidus. Constantine introduced the solidus in 309 CE, and it became the major coin of the Roman monetary system. Modern scholars have dubbed it the "dollar of the Middle Ages."

A New Rome in the East

In the year 324 Constantine defeated Licinius, the emperor of the Eastern Empire, and became sole ruler of both parts of the Roman Empire. Constantine made Byzantium, an ancient city in present-day Turkey, the new capital of the Roman world. He intended this city to be the New Rome, and all state functions were transferred there. Many great buildings were put up, and a splendid city was created.

In one very important respect Constantine's new city was different from Rome: from the outset Byzantium was planned as a Christian city, with three great churches at its center. On May 11, 330, the new city was officially inaugurated and given a new name: Constantinople – named in honor of Constantine the Great. Shortly before his death, in 337, Constantine was baptized. He was buried in Constantinople, a city that remained a major Christian center for the next twelve hundred years.

◀ *The Arch of Constantine (erected 315 CE), in Rome, was built in honor of Constantine's victory over Maxentius. It was a triumphal entryway to the Roman forum, through which victorious generals passed. A Latin inscription carved on the arch states: "Constantine overcame his enemies by divine inspiration."*

SEE ALSO

- Christianity
- Roman Republic and Empire
- Rome, City of

Copán

Copán, a city-state of the Mayan people, was built, probably in the second century CE, in present-day western Honduras, in Central America. The city occupied about 250 acres (100 hectares). Its central district covered 54 acres (22 hectares), and its major buildings date from the height of the Mayan civilization, around 600 CE. Copán was the capital of the region and had its own sovereign, called an *ahau*. The name Copán means "the beautiful, the sweet."

Many of the wonders of Copán still survive. Tall stone monuments known as stelae remain, as they once were, with carved altars for worship at their base. The city had a large center, now called the Acropolis, an area where nobles lived and rituals were carried out. All around Copán were great altars. One altar, known as Altar Q, depicts the life of the founder of Copán, Yax K'uk Mo', who reigned some time between 400 and 500 CE.

Ball Court

Festivals and games played an important part of life in Copán. One of the best pre-served remains at Copán is the Ball Court, an open space with sloped walls on each side. Here the Maya people played a ball game called *palla*, or *pok-ta-pok*. The rules of this game are unknown, but scholars believe that it was an important part of a religious ceremony and not simply a game played for fun.

Writing and Science

Copán contained a school for scribes, and many glyphs (picture symbols used as writing) can still be found there. One struc-ture that survived is known as the Stairway of Hieroglyphs.

The sixty-three steps of this stairway together contain approximately 2,500 glyphs. The Maya used these glyphs (pictorial symbols) as a form of written communication, and they reveal a lot about the scientific and cultural life of the city – Copán was a center for the study of science.

▼ *A plan of the central part of ancient Copán.*

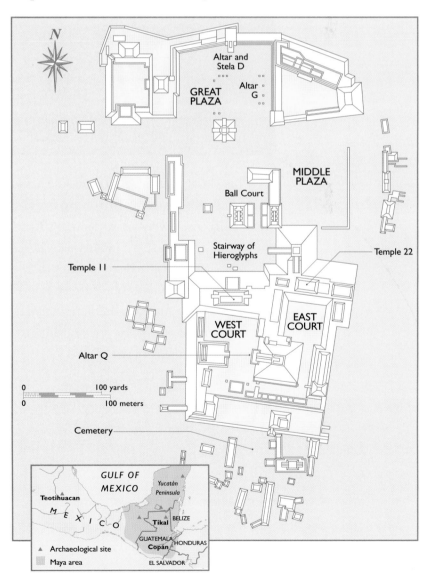

Two rulers seated on glyphs in Temple 11 at Copán. The stone carving shows the ceremony taking place at the accession of King Yax-Pac in 775 CE.

The Maya were skilled astronomers and used their observations of the moon and stars to invent a way of measuring time. They calculated that 149 moons were equal to 4,400 days; thus, their lunar month was very close to 29.53 days, the correct length. The Maya were also talented mathematicians; theirs was one of the few ancient civilizations to use the concept of zero.

JOHN LLOYD STEPHENS, AN AMERICAN TRAVELER AND ARCHAEOLOGIST, WHO FIRST EXPLORED COPÁN IN 1839, IS SAID TO HAVE BOUGHT THE SITE FOR FIFTY DOLLARS. HE WROTE:

[Copán is] a valley of romance and wonder where the genii who attended King Solomon [a Hebrew king famed for his wisdom and his riches] seem to have been artists.

Conclusion

Copán was a fiercely independent city-state, and for much of its history, it successfully defended its borders against neighboring states. However, in 735, Copán was attacked by its neighbor Quirigua, thirty miles (48 km) away. Copán survived until about 800, and then rapidly declined; its final king was Yax Pasah. By the time the Spanish conquistadores arrived in the early 1500s, the great cities of the Maya, including Copán, had long since fallen into ruin.

SEE ALSO

• Maya

Corinth

Corinth was a powerful city-state in ancient Greece. The key to its success was its impressive geographical position. It controlled the land traffic between northern Greece and the Peloponnese in the south. Because of its position on an isthmus (a thin strip of land surrounded by water) – the Saronic Gulf to the east and the Gulf of Corinth to the west – it was also well situated for sea traffic. From the eighth century BCE Corinth established colonies in places such as Corfu and Sicily, and the resulting trade in pottery, metalwork, and cloth brought Corinth immense riches.

At its height the city of Corinth may have had a population of around 100,000. The focal point of the city was the agora, an open marketplace surrounded by government buildings. Excavation has shown that the marketplace was supplied with running water from a source known as the Sacred Spring, which had bronze lions' heads as water spouts. Water was also supplied by the impressive Fountain of Peirene.

On the southern side of the agora was the bema, a platform for making public statements. To the north of the agora stood the Temple of Apollo, dedicated to the god of light, truth, and healing. The temple, with its massive roof supported by a row of Doric columns, contained an entrance hall, a *cella* (an inner shrine), a rear hall used for religious offerings, and a treasury.

Corinth was well provided with buildings for entertainment: a large fourth-century-BCE theater decorated with paintings and a smaller odeon, a semicircular building for musical and poetry recitals. The odeon could hold three thousand spectators and was probably roofed.

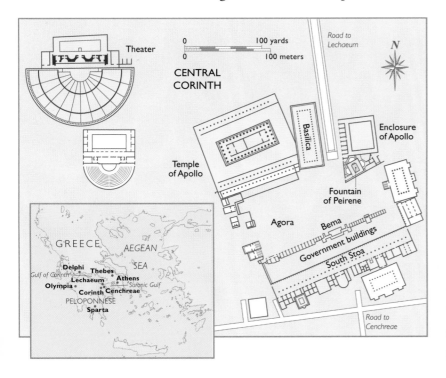

◀ A plan of Corinth. The inset map shows its location in ancient Greece.

Because the sea brought such prosperity to Corinth, the Isthmian Games were founded in 582 BCE in honor of Poseidon, the Greek god of the sea. The games took place in the spring of every second year in a great stadium, where the starting line and holes used by the athletes can still be seen.

The Decline of Corinth

By the second century BCE Greece was being challenged by the rising power of Rome, and in 146 BCE the Roman army totally destroyed Corinth. The city was rebuilt 102 years later by Julius Caesar, who saw its economic potential. Once again trade and commerce thrived.

Around 51 or 52 CE Paul of Tarsus founded a Christian community in Corinth; Paul's Epistles (letters) to the Corinthians are found in the New Testament of the Bible. The emperor Hadrian added more impressive buildings to Corinth between 128 and 134, but they were destroyed by a massive earthquake in 375. Classical Corinth was finally destroyed by the Goths, led by Alaric, in 396.

PERIANDER *c. 625–585 BCE*

Under the leadership of Periander, Corinth enjoyed a period of prosperity and cultural growth. Corinthian black-figure pottery became famous throughout the Greek world, and Corinth's ships traded with distant Egypt. Periander was able to amass great wealth from the traffic across the isthmus. The Corinthians built a *diolkos*, or slipway, that allowed warships and cargoes to be hauled across the isthmus on trolleys pulled by oxen. The Corinthians charged a toll (payment) for this service, and ships were willing to pay it to avoid a longer voyage. The deep ruts caused by the trolley wheels in the stone slipway can still be seen.

SEE ALSO

- Caesar, Julius • Greece, Classical
- Hadrian • Paul of Tarsus

▶ Corinth was one of the richest and most developed cities in ancient Greece. The well-paved main street, shown here, which served the halls, offices, and shops of the agora, was a source of civic pride.

Crime and Punishment

As ancient peoples began to organize themselves into communities, laws were needed so that order and peace could be maintained. The laws were designed to protect both society and individuals. Breaking these laws incurred punishment. These punishments had two basic aims: to deter other people from carrying out similar crimes and to exact revenge upon the criminal for the damage he or she had done.

Societies often wrote down their laws in systematic collections called codes. Historians can study surviving codes to find out what sorts of crimes were being committed in ancient times and what sorts of punishments were carried out.

Babylon

The Code of Hammurabi was one of the earliest lists of laws to have been written down. Hammurabi was the king of Babylon from 1792 to 1750 BCE. In looking at the laws, it appears that murder and assault were common crimes, and the principle of *lex talionis* (the law of retaliation) was laid down, which says "a life for a life." A person found guilty of murder would have to give up his or her own life. However, the code does distinguish between deliberate killing (murder) and accidental killing (manslaughter).

The death penalty was also applied to other crimes, such as bearing false witness (telling lies, often about another person), stealing property from a temple, and even mixing with people known to be criminals. The form of execution varied; individuals found guilty might be drowned, stoned, hanged, or beheaded.

In Hammurabi's time medicine was fraught with danger for both the patient and the physician. The patient's death or the loss of an eye on the operating table could cost the physician his fingers – this punishment is an example of the law of retaliation.

◀ The law code of Hammurabi, king of Babylon, was engraved on this stone pillar, which dates from around 1750 BCE. The carving shows Hammurabi receiving the laws from Shamash, the sun god and god of justice. The pillar was found at Susa in Iran.

A page from a twelfth-century-CE book containing the laws of Moses. It was written by a rabbi called Moses Maimonides (1135–1204) and is called the Mishneh Torah.

Hammurabi had these laws inscribed on stones. On the stone found in the Temple of Shamash at Sippar, Hammurabi states that the purpose of his code was "to promote the welfare of the people...to cause justice to prevail in the land, to destroy the wicked and the evil. That the strong might not oppress the weak."

Mosaic Law

Moses, the Hebrew prophet and lawgiver who lived somewhere around 1300 BCE, laid down a code, known as Mosaic Law. It is found in the Torah, the first five books of the Old Testament of the Bible. There are 613 laws attributed to Moses, the most famous being the Ten Commandments. Mosaic Law, Moses said, sets forth the "laws of God." The code is harsh, and some punishments were severe. If a sacrifice was made to any other god except "the Lord," for example, the guilty party was to be "utterly destroyed." This punishment was thought to be appropriate because the First

Commandment had been broken: "Thou shalt have no other gods before me." The Mosaic code also continues the idea of revenge that was a principle of Babylonian law: "Breach for breach, eye for an eye, tooth for a tooth." The punishments laid down in the Torah for breaking God's laws are precise: burning, stoning, flogging, and amputation of the hand.

The Hittites

By contrast the Hittite Empire of the second millenium BCE, based in southern Anatolia (modern Turkey) and northern Syria, took a different view of punishment. Instead of retribution for serious crime, they insisted on restitution (compensation) to make good any wrong. For example, if a person kills "in anger a man or woman, he must hand over the latter and give four persons." This statement is taken to mean that the price the murderer had to pay the dead person's family was four slaves.

The same principle was applied to the crimes of assault, practicing black magic (sorcery), and theft. A person who injured another by breaking an arm or leg paid a fine of twenty shekels. For killing a merchant, the price a person had to pay was one and a half pounds of silver, and the murderer was then free to continue his life as before. Mutilation – the amputation of limbs, hands, or fingers or disfigurement – was reserved for slaves or people who had directly offended the king.

Greece

The ancient Greeks believed that all leaders received their laws from Zeus, the king of the gods. In about 621 BCE Draco, the Athenian lawgiver, issued a code that punished almost every crime with death. Other penalties depended on the motives of the accused and the level of guilt. Hence, a penalty that is considered unfairly harsh is still said to be draconian.

▼ *Ixion, mythological king of the Lapiths, a mountain tribe in Thessaly, tried to seduce Zeus's wife, Hera. As punishment, Zeus crucified him on a revolving wheel in Hell, where he suffered for eternity.*

CRUCIFIXION

Crucifixion was probably the most brutal punishment practiced in the Roman Empire and Persia. It was used for a variety of crimes from treason to theft. The victim was first beaten and then either bound or nailed to a wooden cross beam fixed to a vertical post in the ground. The cross beams were sometimes attached to trees. Death was horribly slow and usually resulted from blood loss, suffocation, heart failure, or dehydration. Crucified bodies were displayed in public places as a warning to others who might consider breaking the law.

Another punishment used by the Athenian assembly was ostracism, banishment without trial for up to ten years. The word comes from *ostraka*, the broken pieces of pottery on which the names for ostracism were written. It was often used as a punishment for people whose loyalty to Athens was in doubt.

Rome

Roman punishment could be very severe. Nine crimes held the death penalty. Arsonists who set fire to buildings were whipped and then burned, while the punishment for slander was to be be beaten to death with clubs. Later in the Roman Empire, punishments tended to reflect status in society. Important people were either banished or beheaded, while hanging, burning, being buried in mines, or being killed by wild animals in the amphitheater were reserved for the lower orders. Until 43 CE an unpleasant punishment for many criminals in Rome was to be flung from the Tarpeian Rock, a high precipice on the southwest corner of the Capitol. This fate awaited perjurers, those who plotted against the state, or slaves who stole.

SEE ALSO
- Greece, Classical
- Hittites
- Moses
- Roman Republic and Empire

◀ *Any challenges to Roman authority were met with swift and severe punishments. This section of the column of Marcus Aurelius in Rome shows the beheading of German nobles captured in battle.*

Cycladic Culture

The Cyclades are a group of small islands in the southern Aegean Sea. They are so named because of the way they circle around the central holy island of Delos. The people who lived on these islands in the early and middle Bronze Age created a unique and mysterious culture. Little is known about the early Cycladic peoples, as they left no inscriptions or written records. Most of the evidence that exists comes from graves. Archaeologists cannot even agree when the Cycladic people flourished, for they did not stay in their settlements for very long.

Tools and Artifacts

Although the Cycladic people had excellent metalworking skills, they still used stone tools for certain jobs. The finest of these tools were made from polished obsidian, a blue volcanic rock that shimmers like glass, found on the island of Melos. The Cycladic people were skilled potters and made decorated clay vases and jars of all shapes and sizes. The fine white marble found on the island of Paros was soft and easily worked by artisans to make delicate goblets and other table objects. Bronze, an alloy of copper and tin, was used to make a wide range of practical objects such as tweezers, chisels, fishhooks, and daggers. Many pieces of gold jewelry have also been found in Cycladic tombs.

Cycladic Figures

The greatest creations of the early Cycladic age were the marble figurines discovered in tombs at the six-hundred-grave cemetery at Chalandriani on the island of Syros and at other such sites. Many of these figurines are female shapes and may represent the great mother goddess who appears in many Bronze Age religions.

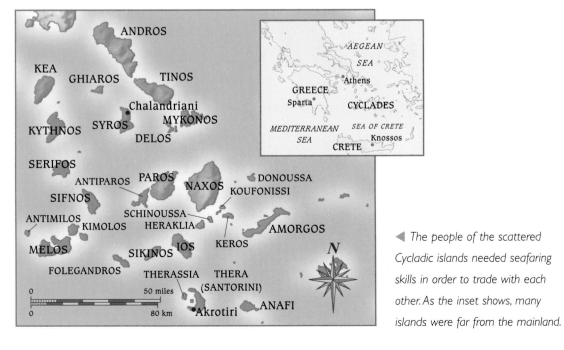

◀ The people of the scattered Cycladic islands needed seafaring skills in order to trade with each other. As the inset shows, many islands were far from the mainland.

AKROTIRI

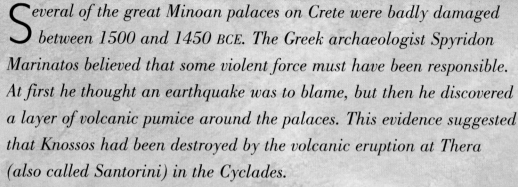

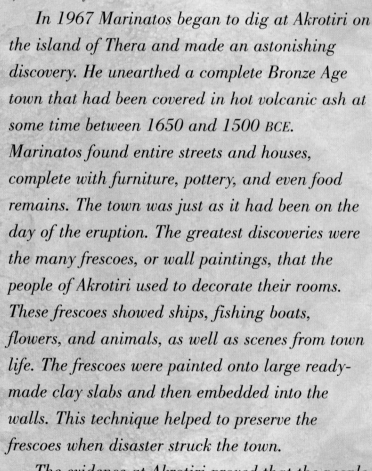

Several of the great Minoan palaces on Crete were badly damaged between 1500 and 1450 BCE. The Greek archaeologist Spyridon Marinatos believed that some violent force must have been responsible. At first he thought an earthquake was to blame, but then he discovered a layer of volcanic pumice around the palaces. This evidence suggested that Knossos had been destroyed by the volcanic eruption at Thera (also called Santorini) in the Cyclades.

In 1967 Marinatos began to dig at Akrotiri on the island of Thera and made an astonishing discovery. He unearthed a complete Bronze Age town that had been covered in hot volcanic ash at some time between 1650 and 1500 BCE. Marinatos found entire streets and houses, complete with furniture, pottery, and even food remains. The town was just as it had been on the day of the eruption. The greatest discoveries were the many frescoes, or wall paintings, that the people of Akrotiri used to decorate their rooms. These frescoes showed ships, fishing boats, flowers, and animals, as well as scenes from town life. The frescoes were painted onto large ready-made clay slabs and then embedded into the walls. This technique helped to preserve the frescoes when disaster struck the town.

The evidence at Akrotiri proved that the people there had many contacts with Minoan Crete and that their town had been destroyed in the same eruption that had also caused considerable damage on Crete. Marinatos was also convinced that the seafaring people of the Cyclades had many links to Libya in North Africa.

▼ Many of the wall paintings at Akrotiri show young men engaged in sports like boxing. These paintings were heavily influenced by Minoan styles and fashions.

CYCLADIC CULTURE

c. 3200 BCE

Beginnings of early Bronze Age culture on the Cyclades.

c. 2600 BCE

Period of Chalandriani tomb figures.

c. 2200 BCE

Evidence of warfare in the Cyclades at Kastri citadel.

c. 1700 BCE

Heavy influence of Crete's Minoan culture on Cyclades.

c. 1500 BCE

Volcanic eruption at Thera (Santorini).

c. 1400 BCE

Cyclades fall under Mycenean control.

c. 1000 BCE

Occupation of the islands by Ionic-speaking Greeks; end of Cycladic Age.

▼ *This delicate figure of a seated harpist was made from fine marble from the Cycladic island of Paros and was discovered on the island of Keros.*

The most complex sculptures are of male musicians, including a seated harpist and a standing flute player. These sculptures may have been idols of Cycladic gods or simply images of the dead. Chalandriani also provided fine examples of the elaborate "frying-pan" clay sculptures that have baffled scholars for over a century. They may have been ritual vases or a kind of mirror for use by the dead in the afterlife.

The End of the Cycladic Culture

From 1700 BCE onward the Cyclades were influenced by the Minoan civilization on Crete. After 1500 BCE new ideas and new settlers came from the north, as the Cyclades became part of the Mycenaean world. Around 1000 BCE the islands were occupied by Ionic Greeks. Delos, home of the gods Apollo and Artemis, became one of the most sacred places in the Mediterranean. The people of the Cyclades began copying Greek styles, and their own ancient culture was forgotten and lost.

A New Appreciation

In the nineteenth century most scholars saw the simple sculptures of the early Cycladic people as primitive and barbaric compared with the art of classical Greece. When the German archaeologist Paul Wolters discovered a life-size Cycladic head in 1891, he dismissed it as "repulsively ugly." However, ideas about art changed a great deal in the twentieth century. For instance, the sculptor Brancusi was inspired by the rounded shapes of Cycladic figures to create his own masterpieces. In the twenty-first century the beautiful simplicity of these Cycladic treasures continues to be appreciated.

SEE ALSO

- Knossos • Minoans
- Mycenaean Civilization

Cyrus the Great

Cyrus II (c. 590–529 BCE), known as Cyrus the Great, is traditionally regarded as the fourth of the Achaemenid kings and the founder of the Persian Empire. According to the Greek historian Herodotus, Cyrus's grandfather was Astyages, king of the Medes, who had dreamed that he would lose his throne to his grandson. Astyages ordered one of his servants to kill the infant, but the servant's wife secretly reared the boy, who grew into a wise leader of men. In 559 BCE Cyrus became king of Anshan, at that time under the rule of the Medes. Then in 550 BCE he united the Persians and the Medes under his rule and reduced his grandfather to a mere prisoner at his court.

Conquest of Lydia

In 547 BCE the Persian Empire was attacked by the kingdom of Lydia in western Anatolia. After a brief skirmish the Lydians retreated to their capital of Sardis. Cyrus followed and met them in battle beneath the walls of Sardis. The Lydians were excellent horsemen, and the long spears of their cavalrymen were the greatest asset of their army. Cyrus is said to have ordered his men to ride into battle mounted on camels. The smell of the Persian camels disturbed the horses of the Lydians and threw their army into confusion. The Lydians retreated behind the high walls and cliffs of Sardis. One of Cyrus's men spotted a Lydian soldier who dropped his helmet and climbed down the cliffs to fetch it. By doing so, the soldier revealed to the Persians a route through the city's defenses and enabled them to capture the city.

Religious Freedom

Cyrus knew that his vast empire, which stretched from the Mediterranean to the Hindu Kush, contained many different peoples. He knew he could rule them peacefully only if he governed with their consent. He respected the many different gods worshiped by his subjects. When his troops captured Babylon in 539 BCE, Cyrus made sure that the Temple of Marduk was protected. He freed the Jews from their long slavery in Babylon, and forty thousand returned to Judah.

◀ *A bas-relief of a winged spirit guarding one of the gateways of the palace of Cyrus at Pasargadae. The form of the figure unites traditions from different parts of the empire. The dress is Babylonian, the form of the wings is Assyrian, the beard is in the Persian style, and the headdress is a divine crown of Egypt.*

Pasargadae

Cyrus built a new capital at Pasargadae. Stonemasons from across Asia were summoned to build the city in the plain of Morghab. The buildings were a strange mix of Greek, Babylonian, Assyrian, Egyptian, and Persian designs.

Cyrus died in 529 BCE fighting the tribes of central Asia. He had already built his tomb at Pasargadae, a small, simple building on top of a platform of plain stone steps. According to the Roman historian Arrian, Alexander the Great ordered the restoration of the tomb after reading the inscription: "O man, I am Cyrus, who founded the empire of the Persians and was king of Asia. Grudge me not this monument." The tomb has survived, although there is no trace of the inscription.

WHEN THE PERSIANS CAPTURED BABYLON IN 539 BCE, CYRUS ORDERED HIS TROOPS TO TREAT THE CITY AND ITS INHABITANTS WITH RESPECT. THE PEOPLE OF THE CITY ARE SAID TO HAVE WELCOMED THEIR NEW RULER INTO THE CITY WITH ENTHUSIASM.

All the inhabitants of Babylon, as well as the entire country of Sumer and Akkad, princes and governors, bowed to Cyrus and kissed his feet, jubilant that he had received the kingship, and with shining faces they happily greeted him as a master through whose help they had come to life from death and had all been spared damage and disaster, and they worshiped his name.

FROM AN INSCRIPTION ON A CLAY CYLINDER WRITTEN IN AKKADIAN

SEE ALSO
- Achaemenids
- Aryans
- Babylon
- Babylonians
- Hebrews
- Herodotus
- Jerusalem
- Marduk
- Nebuchadrezzar II

▶ *Although he was one of the greatest kings of the ancient world, Cyrus ordered that he be buried in a plain, simple stone tomb.*

Darius I

Darius (548–486 BCE), the Greek form of the old Persian name Daryavahvsh, won the throne of Persia by a mixture of trickery and force. In 521 BCE he helped to murder the magus, or high priest, Gaumata, who had pretended to be the true king of Persia. In his first years as king, Darius had to crush several revolts throughout the empire. Unlike Cyrus the Great, however, Darius dealt severely with his rebellious subjects. When he recaptured Babylon after a long siege, three thousand leading Babylonians were impaled to show that Darius was again master of the city.

One Empire

Darius wanted to unite his far-flung lands into one effective empire. He divided his territories into twenty provinces, each under a Persian satrap, or governor. To check the power of the satraps, the army in each province was led by men who were totally loyal to Darius. Other royal officials, such as messengers and tax collectors, acted as the king's ears. They reported back each year to the king's advisers at the royal city of Susa. Unlike Cyrus, who apparently allowed his subjects to worship their own local gods, Darius may have set up a new state religion. Ahura Mazda was now the supreme god and "wise lord" of Persia.

▼ A satrap, or provincial governor, pays homage to Darius on his throne at Persepolis. The precious gifts brought by the satraps were stored in the royal treasury there.

Darius needed to know what was going
on in the distant satrapies. He also needed
to be able to send troops quickly to any part
of the empire. He therefore built a road that
ran for 1,680 miles (2,704 km) from Susa
to distant Sardis, near the Aegean coast.
Fresh horses were stabled at over 110 relay
stations along the route. Darius also built
two canals in Egypt to link the Nile delta
and the Mediterranean with the Red Sea.

Wars with the Scythians and Greeks

Sometime between 520 and 513 BCE,
Darius conquered the Punjab region of
India, and by 517 he controlled the Ionian
Islands in the Aegean. Around 515 Darius
set out to defeat the Scythian tribes who
lived in southeastern Europe. He trans-
ported his men across the Bosporus, the sea
strait between Europe and Asia, on a bridge
of boats tied together. On this campaign
Darius reached deep into Europe, march-
ing to the banks of the Danube and the
Volga and adding Thrace and Macedon to
his empire.

In the 490s his Greek subjects in Ionia
rebelled against him. The rebels were
helped by the Greek city of Athens. In
490 BCE Darius sent a huge army and fleet
to punish the Athenians. However, the
Athenians and their allies from the city of
Plataea launched a surprise attack on the
Persians while their ships lay in the bay of
Marathon. Over 6,400 Persians were killed,
while the Greeks lost fewer than 200 men.
Darius was to die before he could launch
another expedition against the troublesome
Greeks.

SEE ALSO
- Achaemenids
- Ahura Mazda
- Aryans
- Athens • Babylon
- Herodotus
- Indus Valley
- Persepolis
- Scythians
- Zoroastrianism

▲ A bull sculpture at the ruins of the palace at
Persepolis. Visitors were carefully guided past huge
sculptures and towering columns into the vast audience
hall called the Apadana. Here three thousand subjects
bowed before the king on his throne.

David

David (c. 1040–965 BCE) was born in the village of Bethlehem and belonged to the tribe of Judah. According to the Bible, David was the greatest of the early Israelite rulers, the king who united the tribes of Israel and Judah and created a true nation-state.

David and Saul

As a young man, David came to the notice of Saul, the first king of Israel. According to one story in the Bible, David, a shepherd boy, killed the giant Philistine champion, Goliath, with a stone hurled from a sling.

David became Saul's son-in-law and a successful general. However, his popularity aroused the jealousy of Saul, who plotted to kill him. David fled to the wilderness, living as an outlaw with a growing army of followers. The Philistines, another people contesting for rule of the region, then won a great victory over the Israelites, killing Saul and three of his sons.

With Saul gone, the Israelites were desperate for strong leadership. They turned to David, who had already proved his skill in war. He was acclaimed king, first of his own tribe of Judah and then of the northern kingdom, Israel.

Jerusalem

David's greatest achievement, around 1000 BCE, was to capture Jerusalem and make it his royal capital. Jerusalem was an ancient hill town then occupied by a people called the Jebusites. It was an ideal capital because of its central position between Judah and Israel and because it had never belonged to one particular tribe. David made his city a center for religious worship by placing the Ark of the Covenant there. This was the wooden chest that held the Ten Commandments and that represented God's presence.

Final Years

David led his armies in a series of successful wars. He ended the power of the Philistines by limiting them to a coastal plain on the Mediterranean Sea, then he conquered all his neighbors. His last years were troubled, as he was forced to put down several rebellions

▶ *This famous statue of David, by the Italian artist Michelangelo (1475–1564), shows him moments before his duel with Goliath. With his sling resting on his left shoulder, he gazes at Goliath, judging the distance between them.*

against him, one by his favorite son, Absalom. David died at the age of seventy, after ruling for forty years.

Did David's Empire Exist?

According to the Bible, David ruled a mighty empire stretching from the Dead Sea to Anatolia (Turkey). Archaeologists have spent many years searching for evidence of David's empire but have found none. There is no mention of David in Egyptian or Hittite sources. In the time of David, Jerusalem seems to have been a small hill town and not the capital of an empire. Many experts believe that the Bible stories, which took their final form centuries after David lived, must have exaggerated the king's power.

David was such an important figure in Jewish history that all later kings claimed descent from him. When the Jews came to hope for a messiah (anointed one) to restore the kingdom, they expected him to come

He destroyed the enemies on every side, and brought to nothing the Philistines his enemies ... In all his works he praised the Holy One most high with words of glory; with his whole heart he sang songs, and loved him that made him.

ECCLESIASTICUS 47: 7–8 (KJV)

from the family of David. The prophet Micah predicted that, like David, the messiah would be born in Bethlehem.

Because David was said to be a musician, he was also given credit for writing the collection of holy songs known as the Book of Psalms. In fact most of the psalms date from a much later period.

SEE ALSO
- Hebrews
- Jerusalem
- Jesus of Nazareth
- Moses

▼ *Stories of David inspired Christian artists for hundreds of years. This fourteenth-century French tapestry shows David bringing the Ark of the Covenant to Jerusalem. As in all medieval art, the people wear clothes of the artist's own time.*

Dead Sea Scrolls

In 1947 an Arab boy named Muhammad edh-Dhib made one of the most important and exciting archaeological discoveries of the twentieth century. While searching for a lost goat in the hills overlooking the Dead Sea, he found a cave full of pottery jars that contained scrolls – books made of rolls of sheepskin, covered in ancient writing. Later, ten more caves containing scrolls were found nearby.

This find amounted to an ancient library and included twelve complete scrolls and 801 works surviving in fragments. The scrolls were made between 300 BCE and 70 CE and include copies of books of the Hebrew Bible, commentaries on sacred books, hymns, prayers, calendars, and rule books for a religious community.

Where Did They Come From?

The great mystery of the scrolls is, who wrote them, and why were they hidden in caves and never recovered? One theory is that they belonged to a Jewish sect called the Essenes, who were said to live in the desert like monks. Archaeologists who excavated a neighboring group of ruins, at Qumran, suggested that Qumran was the site of the Essene "monastery" that had produced the texts.

Another idea is that the scrolls came from Jerusalem, which was sacked by the Romans in 70 CE. Evidence for this theory is an unusual scroll, written on a sheet of copper, that lists buried treasure, including twenty-six tons (23,587 kg) of gold and sixty-five tons (58,967 kg) of silver. So much wealth could not have belonged to a desert community. It is more likely that it came from the temple in Jerusalem. At least some of the scrolls may also have been brought from the city by Jews fleeing from the advancing Romans.

The Significance of the Scrolls

The scrolls preserve copies of Bible texts that are a thousand years older than any previously known. As these texts exist in different versions, it seems clear that in the first century CE there was still no fixed

◀ This copper scroll listing buried treasures is the most mysterious of all those found. Many people have searched for the treasure, without success. The scroll had to be cut into pieces before it could be opened.

Hebrew Bible. Instead there were varying versions of the holy books, all of which the Jews took care to preserve. This finding has added a new understanding to the history of the Bible.

Equally important is the light the scrolls throw on early Christianity. There are many parallels between the scroll community and the first Christians. Both groups described themselves as "sons of light." The community members, like early Christians, believed that they were living in the end of time, when Bible prophecies would be fulfilled. They expected a messiah, sent by God, to save the faithful. In one scroll the messiah is described as a lord who would "restore sight to the blind, revive the dead, and bring good news to the poor." The key difference between the two groups is that the Christians believed the messiah had already come, in the person of Jesus.

▲ Some archaeologists have argued that this ruined building at Qumran was the scriptorium (writing room) where the scrolls were written. Yet there is no firm evidence linking Qumran with the scrolls. The mystery of their source remains.

SEE ALSO
- Hebrews
- Jesus of Nazareth
- Judaism • Masada

ONE OF THE SCROLLS DESCRIBES A FINAL BATTLE BETWEEN THE "CHILDREN OF LIGHT" AND THE FORCES OF EVIL – THE "CHILDREN OF DARKNESS." IT GIVES INSTRUCTIONS FOR THE BATTLE ORDER AND EVEN INSCRIPTIONS TO BE DISPLAYED AT DIFFERENT STAGES OF THE BATTLE:

The first division shall hurl seven javelins of war towards the enemy formation. On the point of the javelins they shall write, "Shining Javelin of the Power of God"; and on the darts of the second division they shall write, "Bloody Spikes to Bring Down the Slain by the Wrath of God."

THE WAR SCROLL

Death and Burial

The oldest graves in the world are 400,000 years old. They were discovered near Beijing in China. It was, however, the Neanderthal people, living between 100,000 and 30,000 years ago, who showed the first signs of a belief in life after death.

The Neanderthals buried their dead inside the caves they lived in, often close to the fire. The intention was to keep their dead relatives warm and preserve signs of life for as long as possible. Tools and weapons were placed in the graves, as well as food, including joints of meat. The Neanderthals clearly believed that the dead had needs similar to those of the living. The corpses were often arranged to look like they were sleeping, especially when whole families were buried together. Some were interred with their knees drawn up to their chin, like babies waiting to be reborn.

The Land of No Return

The Mesopotamians did not believe in rebirth. Instead they believed that everyone, good and bad, faced the same terrible fate after death. The dead went to live in a dark place called the underworld, or "the land of no return."

The gate to the underworld was guarded by scorpion people, who made sure no one living could enter to save friends or relatives. A clerk named Dimpimekug wrote down the names of all new arrivals in the Book of the Dead. The land of no return was built inside a mountain, where it was too dark to see anything. The people living there ate dust or clay and wore wings instead of clothes.

The eternal darkness of the land awaiting them did not stop the Mesopotamian kings from trying to lead a privileged life beyond the grave. They were buried in huge underground warrens surrounded by the belongings they might need in the underworld. Their bodies were laid out in a comfortable sleeping position. The slaves and servants of the royal household were buried with them in a kneeling position, ready to spring to attention when they and their masters woke up.

▼ The royals of Sumer believed they would live in luxury even after death. These pieces of precious jewelry, dating from around 2500 BCE, were found in Queen Pu-Abi's grave in Ur. They belonged to one of her attendants, buried with her.

THE COLORS OF DEATH

The Neanderthals sprinkled red ocher on the bodies of the dead. The color was a symbol of warmth and life. Egyptians considered black the color of life because it was the color of Nile mud, the substance that gave Egypt its life. Anubis, the god of mummification, was always drawn in black to remind people of what he stood for.

The Greeks wore black when they were in mourning. The Romans held their funerals in the dark of night. However, the ancient Hebrews wrapped their dead in white linen, a symbol of purity and humility. White remains the traditional color of mourning in China and Japan.

The Kingdom of Osiris

The Egyptian view of life after death was far more hopeful. They believed that good people went to live in the kingdom of Osiris, a wonderful world that was a mirror image of Egypt itself.

To make sure that a person enjoyed the afterlife, the Egyptians buried their dead with food, drink, clothing, jewelry, and anything else that had brought pleasure in life. Egyptian embalmers took great care to preserve the corpse. The brain was removed and apparently discarded, and the liver, lungs, stomach, and intestines were placed in special canopic jars. The heart was left in the body to be weighed by the gods. The body was dried out with natron salt and wrapped in bandages to make a mummy.

▼ This was the mummy case of Nespanetjerenpere, a priest of the god Amun. It dates from some time between the tenth and eighth centuries BCE and is made of linen or papyrus, mixed with plaster, and decorated with paint and glass.

Before the burial the Egyptian priests performed a ceremony called "the opening of the mouth" so that the dead person could speak again in the afterlife and use all five senses. The mummy was then sealed in a coffin called a sarcophagus and buried on the west bank of the Nile facing east toward the rising sun to help his or her spirit to be reborn.

To join the gods, a dead Egyptian person had to go through an underworld called Duat, which was full of tests and obstacles that had to be overcome. The final challenge took place in the Hall of Two Truths, where the gods weighed the dead person's heart against a magical feather. If the heart and feather balanced, the person was judged to have led a good life, and he or she was allowed to join the great god Osiris in his kingdom. If the person failed because their heart was heavy with sin, the heart was eaten by a monster called Ammut.

Tartaros

Like the Egyptians, the ancient Greeks also believed in the land of the dead. The Greeks called it Tartaros. In the afterlife good people were rewarded with a happy existence, while the bad suffered eternal punishment. To get to Tartaros, a dead soul had to pass by a three-headed dog called Cerberus. For the price of a coin, a boatman called Charon would ferry the dead person across the River Styx. Pluto and Persephone, the gods of the dead, waited to judge new arrivals to the underworld.

Most Greeks cremated their dead before burying them. The ashes were put in special urns. During the Hellenistic period (323–31 BCE), burial of the whole body became more popular. To make sure their dead relatives would cross the Styx, the ancient Greeks used to put a coin in the person's grave. Rich people also gave the deceased burial gifts, including jewelry, food, drink, and a special vase called a *lekythos*.

Resurrection

The Romans, whose culture was heavily influenced by the Greeks, also burned their dead. The custom survived in the Roman Empire until the spread of Christianity. The early Christians believed that Jesus, the founder of their religion, would raise them from the dead on judgment day at the end of the world. Corpses had to be left uncremated to be ready for his call. Early Christians were buried in multiple underground caves called catacombs, many of them built in the ground beneath the city of Rome.

◄ This Greek funerary urn, made of bronze, was originally a receptacle for holding water. It dates from the fourth century BCE.

▲ *This marble relief is part of a Roman sarcophagus. It shows Charon ferrying the souls of the dead across the River Styx, the river of the dead. The Romans, who inherited most of their beliefs from the Greeks, were buried with a coin in their mouth to pay Charon.*

Between the fourth century BCE and the second century CE, the Hebrews developed a belief in resurrection – the idea that God brings a person back to life after his or her death. The Hebrew prophets Isaiah and Daniel both wrote about the dead being awakened by God to face judgment for their deeds in life. This belief was inherited by Christianity. Christians believe that Jesus was resurrected three days after his death on the cross. They believe that one day he will return all the dead to life.

INSCRIPTION ON AN EARLY CHRISTIAN GRAVESTONE FROM THE BEGINNING OF THE FOURTH CENTURY CE:

Eutychius, sweetest son, this stone was erected by his father Eutychainus. The child who lived one year, two months, and four days, was the servant of God.

Deborah

Deborah was an Israelite leader who lived in the late second millenium BCE. This was a period when the Israelites were not a nation but belonged to separate scattered tribes that were frequently at war with their neighbors.

In past times of great danger, strong leaders had sometimes come forward to save their tribe or group of tribes from the enemy. Such a leader was called a *shophet*, a word usually translated as "judge" but also meaning "war chieftain" or "decision maker."

Deborah was the only woman to be a *shophet*. Part of her prestige came from the fact that she was also thought to be a prophetess. People believed that Deborah spoke with the authority of Yahweh (God), who had chosen her as his mouthpiece.

Deborah's Prophecy

Only one incident in Deborah's life is well known; it is recorded in the Bible's Book of Judges. According to the story, Deborah was sitting one day beneath a palm tree

▶ This nineteenth-century engraving shows Deborah as an inspired prophetess. Eyes closed, she points her right hand towards the heavens, indicating that her words come directly from God.

where the Israelites came to ask her to solve their disputes. Deborah summoned a man named Barak and told him to take an army and attack the enemy Canaanites, promising him a great victory. Barak agreed to go but only if Deborah went with him. Deborah agreed but prophesied that Barak would not have the honor of the victory. God would hand over the enemy commander, Sisera, to a woman. In the battle that followed, Barak's warriors killed all the Canaanites except for Sisera, who ran away, taking refuge in the tent of a woman named Jael. While Sisera slept, Jael killed him by driving a tent peg into his head and thus fulfilled Deborah's prophecy.

In the Bible the whole story is told as a song of triumph, supposedly sung by Deborah. This victory song is thought to be one of the very oldest parts of the Bible and may even date from Deborah's own time. One sign of its great age is the fact that sections of it are very confused. Such confusion would be expected if it had been handed down from generation to generation.

SEE ALSO

- Hebrews
- Judaism

THE ROLE OF WOMEN

Israel, like most ancient societies, was dominated by men, who could have as many wives as they chose. A woman was expected to obey her father and her husband. A wife called her husband baal (master) and adon (lord). Both Deborah and Jael are first introduced as wives.

Women worked hard in the fields, where they looked after the flocks, and at home, where they spun and wove wool, prepared meals, and cared for children. Hard work even influenced the choice of female names. The name Deborah means "bee"; it might be chosen by parents to encourage a daughter to be as busy as a bee.

Despite their lower status, women, like Deborah, with strong personalities could be respected and influential, even though they could not lead armies. Deborah, for example, had to select Barak to lead the attack. Even so, her importance is shown in the story by the fact that Barak refused to go into battle unless she went with him.

◀ Throughout the ancient world, women lived similar lives. Deborah would have kneaded dough to make bread, just as this pottery figure of a woman from Greece is doing.

Delphi

In central Greece, on the side of Mount Parnassus, lies Delphi, one of the most famous religious sites in the ancient world. Regarded by the ancient Greeks as the exact center of the world and marked by the omphalos (navel stone), Delphi was also the home of the oracle.

When the ancients wanted to know what might happen in the future or if they wished to seek advice on a correct course of action, they consulted the gods. The reply they received and the holy place or shrine they visited to hear it was called an oracle.

The Oracle

The Delphic oracle was special because Apollo, the god of light, truth, and healing, was its master. According to legend, Apollo had killed a terrible beast, called the Python, that lived in the hills near the site of the oracle. From that time onward, the oracles spoken by the priestess of the oracle, whose name was Pythia, were seen as the wisdom of Apollo.

The leaders of the Greek city-states often came to consult the oracle before waging war, setting up new colonies, or siting new cities. Sometimes individuals would come for advice about personal problems. The priestess, seated on a sacred tripod, went into a frenzy, and her prophecies were recorded by a priest who put them into verse.

The Pythian games, held every four years after around 590 BCE, were a celebration of Apollo's victory over the Python and, along with the Olympic games, were the most important competition in the Greek world. Wrestling, running, and throwing events were held at the stadium at Delphi, while chariot races took place on the nearby plain of Krisa.

The Sanctuary

The sacred precinct at Delphi was hugely impressive, containing statues, temples, treasuries, altars, staircases, chambers, and a

▶ A plan of Delphi. The inset shows its location in ancient Greece.

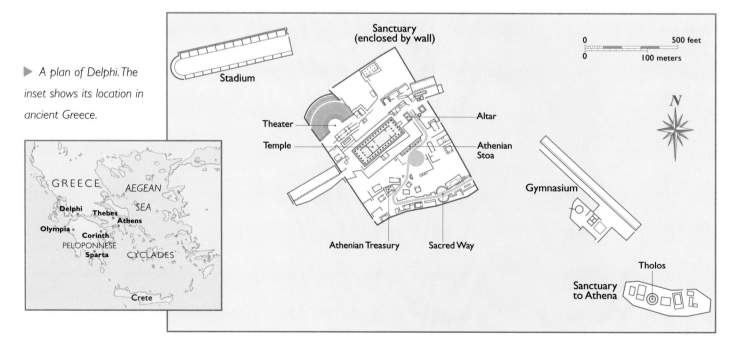

▲ *The Tholos in the sanctuary of Athena Pronoas, at Delphi, dates from around 380 BCE. It was built entirely of marble, and the roof was supported by twenty columns. Its purpose is unknown.*

theater, all reached by a road called the Sacred Way. Before entering, pilgrims washed themselves at a fountain flowing out of three carved lions' heads.

The focal point of the sanctuary was the Temple of Apollo, rebuilt in the fourth century BCE, which contained the chamber of the priestess and the oracle itself. Pilgrims seeking advice sat in a side room separated by a curtain and could consider the wise sayings written on the walls, such as "Know thyself" and "Nothing in excess."

The twenty treasuries of the Greek city-states were sited at various points along the Sacred Way. They were filled with valuable goods (often gold or silver) left there as offerings to Apollo. Looted treasure from defeated enemies was laid out in front of them.

Decline

Under Roman control the sanctuary was looted, and it was badly damaged by the Goths in 396 CE. Delphi was finally closed down in 426 by the Christian Roman emperor Theodosius, who disapproved of pagan beliefs and rituals.

CROESUS, LAST KING OF LYDIA *DIED C. 546 BCE*

Advice from the oracle had to be treated with caution, as it often had a number of possible meanings. The fate of Croesus illustrates this point. King Croesus of Lydia was one of the richest men in the world. He gave huge offerings to Delphi from his gold mines. Cyrus, the Persian leader, threatened Lydia, so Croesus consulted the oracle. It told him, "If Croesus goes to war, he will destroy a great empire." Believing this sentence meant that his victory was assured, Croesus went to war with Persia, only to suffer total defeat. He did not realize that the empire he would destroy was his own.

SEE ALSO

• Cyrus the Great • Greece, Classical • Greek Mythology

Dong Son Culture

The Dong Son civilization developed from earlier cultures who lived in the central part of what is now Vietnam and appeared around 800 BCE. Centered around the Tonkin delta and southward along the coast bordering the China Sea, it lasted for some six hundred years. The Dong Son, who were skilled farmers, metalworkers, and seafarers, spread their influence over much of Southeast Asia. They are considered Vietnam's first great civilization and were responsible for establishing much of Vietnam's culture.

Bronze and Iron

The Dong Son flourished in the later stages of the Bronze Age and the start of the Iron Age. Bronze is an alloy – a mixture of several metals – and in ancient times it was usually made from copper and tin. Large amounts of these metals could be found in the Vietnamese soil. The Dong Son became expert at using bronze to produce jars, ornaments, drums, weapons, and farming tools, such as plows and scythes. Between 600 and 500 BCE the Dong Son also started to work with iron, using it to make weapons and some farm implements. Bronze continued to be worked by the Dong Son long after the introduction of iron.

Skilled Farmers

The Dong Son were an agricultural people; almost all of them were engaged in farming. They kept pigs and buffalo for their meat and also used buffalo and oxen to help drag plows across their fields. The most important part of the Dong Son's diet was rice. The Dong Son were pioneers of wet rice growing. This technique involved growing rice in paddies, which are sectioned-off ponds filled knee-deep with water. Wet rice growing called for large numbers of people to work together to direct the river flow using barriers, called dykes, and to maintain the paddies.

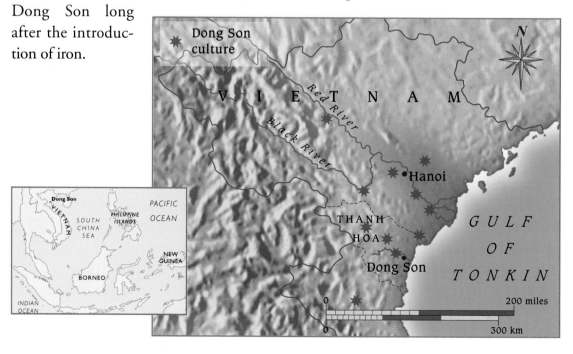

▶ The large map shows the centers of Dong Son culture, which flourished for over seven hundred years.

DONG SON CULTURE

8000–800 BCE

Neolithic Age. Ancestors of Dong Son live in central Vietnam.

c. 800 BCE

Start of the Dong Son civilization centered around the Tonkin delta in Vietnam.

300–200 BCE

Chinese influence in the region increasing.

200–100 BCE

Conquest of the region by several waves of Chinese forces.

111 BCE

Region under the control of the Chinese Han Empire.

▶ *This ax head is from the later period of Dong Son culture, between 200 BCE and 200 CE. It was cast in bronze and decorated with simple geometric designs.*

INFLUENCING INDONESIA

The Dong Son's influence extended beyond Vietnam, as they traveled and traded throughout much of Southeast Asia. They particularly influenced the many islands that make up Indonesia. The Dong Son introduced their bronze-casting and wet rice-growing methods to Indonesia. Indonesian peoples are famous for producing a type of cloth made from dyed threads known as warp-ikat. This too is believed to have been a Dong Son invention.

Water Travelers

The Dong Son often lived near the water, by the riverside or close to the coast, and built houses on bamboo stilts to avoid flooding. They added variety to their diet by becoming skilled fishermen. Historians believe that the Dong Son occasionally used rafts made of lengths of stout bamboo poles lashed together. These rafts may have been used to travel along the region's many rivers and swamplands. The Dong Son's main type of boat was a long, carved, wooden canoe.

The Dong Son were skilled sailors; they traveled large distances by water and visited most of Southeast Asia. Dong Son artifacts have been found in present-day Cambodia, Myanmar, Thailand, Indonesia, and a number of provinces of China. Forces from China finally conquered the Dong Son in the second century BCE, but by then their influence had spread throughout Vietnam and Southeast Asia.

BRONZE DRUMS

The greatest artistic achievements of the Dong Son were undoubtedly their beautiful bronze drums, which are considered artistic masterpieces. The drums required advanced knowledge of metallurgy and great technical skill to heat and mix the metals to the right temperatures and to fashion the clay molds and clay core that made the drums hollow.

Apart from being magnificent works of art, the drums tell much about the Dong Son's lives and religious beliefs. Many scenes carved onto the drums show people at work, pounding rice and building boats, as well as participating in rituals and festivals. The drums may have been used at these festivals along with other instruments of the time, such as cymbals and a khene, an instrument made of several flutes tied together. Leaders used the drums to inspire warriors and call people to battle.

Scenes on drums and other artifacts show drums being carried at the back of a boat filled with warriors.

Although many hundreds of the drums were destroyed when the ancient Chinese invaded, over 140 bronze drums have been unearthed in Vietnam, and others have been located in China, Thailand, and Indonesia. Of all the Dong Son drums recovered, the Ngoc Lu drum is considered the most important. It is exceptionally well preserved, and its detailed decoration of festivals, houses, and animals is clearly visible. Twenty-five inches (64 cm) high and thirty-one inches (79 cm) in diameter, the drum was discovered by accident in 1893.

▼ This bronze drum from the Dong Son civilization was found in Thanh Hoa province and dates from between 300 and 100 BCE. It features two metal hoops for a carrying strap.

SEE ALSO
• China

Glossary

amphitheater An oval, open-air space surrounded by seating, used for public entertainments.

amulet A piece of jewelry worn in ancient times to ward off bad luck.

apostle One of the twelve followers of Jesus, also called disciples.

Asia Minor A peninsula in the extreme west of Asia, roughly corresponding to Asian Turkey.

astrology The study of the positions of the moon, sun, and other planets in the belief that their motions affect human beings.

barbarian A member of a wild, uncivilized people. The word was coined by the Greeks to describe people whose language sounded like "bar, bar."

black-figure pottery Pottery on which the outline of a picture was first painted with slip, a watered-down mixture of clay and ash. The details were then scratched through. In the firing process, the slip baked black, while the rest of the pot turned red, including the scratched detail.

canopic jars Jars used in ancient Egypt to hold the embalmed internal organs of a mummy.

cella The most sacred part of a temple or shrine, often containing the cult statue.

embalmer One who treats a dead body with preservative substances to stop it from decaying.

fresco Wall painting where paint is applied to fresh damp plaster.

gladiator A highly trained fighter, who may have been a slave, a prisoner of war, or a volunteer.

hierarchy A system arranged in ranks according to authority or social position.

hieroglyph Symbol in a system of picture writing used by the Egyptians, the Maya, and other ancient civilizations. Individual hieroglyphs could stand for objects, concepts, or sounds.

Ionia Part of the western Anatolian coast and islands in the Aegean Sea, mostly populated by Greeks, that formed a province of the empire of Darius.

kohl A black powder often used in stick form to paint around the eyes.

Lydia A kingdom of fabulous wealth that occupied much of western Anatolia.

magus A high priest of the Persians especially skilled in interpreting dreams.

Medes A nomadic people related to the Persians and speaking an Indo-European language. They settled most of northern Iran perhaps around 1300 BCE.

metallurgy The techniques and knowledge required to extract and work with metals.

Neanderthal Member of an extinct subspecies of human being that lived in Europe, northern Africa, and western Asia in the early Stone Age.

Nile delta A great triangular area in Egypt where the River Nile flows into the Mediterranean. In ancient times the Nile delta had seven branches.

ocher A natural brownish yellow powder containing rust.

ostracism Exclusion of a person from a social group as a punishment.

pagan A follower of an ancient, polytheistic religion (that is, one involving many gods).

praetorian guard The emperor's personal bodyguard, numbering several thousand soldiers with two commanders.

prophet A person who interprets the will of God.

Republic The period of ancient Roman history between 510 and 27 BCE when Rome was governed by elected representatives of the people, not by an emperor.

rhetoric The art of speaking persuasively.

sarcophagus A stone container used to hold the body of a dead person.

shekel A unit of weight and coinage used by the Babylonians, Hittites, and Jews.

strait A narrow channel of water that joins two larger bodies of water.

Ten Commandments In the Bible, the ten laws given by God to Moses.

Index

Page numbers in **boldface type** refer to main articles.
Page numbers in *italic type* refer to illustrations.